Get into bed with Google

Top ranking search optimisation techniques

Jon Smith

brilliantideas

CAREFUL NOW

There are both good and bad sources of information available on the Internet, in the telephone directory and advertised on bad photocopies for 20 pence a week in the local newsagents. The Internet, especially, is a constantly changing phenomenon and therefore good (and bad) sites are forever popping up and dropping off. Web addresses change, so if a link doesn't work, be sure to use Google to try and find its new home or a similar service offered by another firm or individual. Likewise, you should have an up-to-date virus checker installed before you visit new sites and download anything whatsoever. You should also be aware that new applications may squabble and bicker over who's the daddy – they might not work because of other things you have installed on your machine. We're very sorry about all this and wish it was a better world, but it's the only one we have. We believe in taking it on the chin like grown-ups and expect you to do the same. We love you dearly but if it all goes kumquat shaped then you're on your own; we take no liability. See it as an adventure.

First published in 2008 by
Infinite Ideas Limited
36 St Giles
Oxford
OX1 3LD
United Kingdom
www.infideas.com

Updated reprint 2009

A CIP catalogue record for this book is available from the British Library

ISBN 978-1-905940-49-3

Brand and product names are trademarks or registered trademarks of their respective owners.

Designed and typeset by Baseline Arts Ltd, Oxford
Cover designed by Cylinder
Printed and bound in Great Britain by TJ International Ltd, Padstow, Cornwall

Brilliant ideas

Introduction

There's having a website and there's having a website that works. It's all very well having a flash intro, a fully integrated shopping basket and lots of features and functionality that can wow your audience on every single page. But what if they can't find you? What if you're not visible on the search engines, and on Google in particular? If they don't know your address (which most users don't) then many members of your potential audience are going to try and find your site by typing in a keyword or phrase – and if you don't rank on those return results, you may as well not have a website at all. It's that serious.

Making your site Google friendly or employing search engine optimisation techniques (SEO, as it's known in the trade) at your earliest convenience should be a priority; SEO is this year's black. What it can cost varies wildly, so be sure to question the worth of both the cheapest and most expensive service providers, but remember there's lots that can be done internally and with minimum cost, other than your time. This book will show you what needs to be done and will empower you to ask your SEO service provider – and yourself – the right questions.

To ignore search engine optimisation (and Google in particular) is folly. Having your own website means you simply must get involved with SEO techniques. Without any SEO input, well, if I were a betting man (which I'm not), I'd say your chances of success were about even; if I were an Internet project manager (which I am), I would say you were dead in the water. Your site is nothing if it isn't optimised for the web. In fact, to ignore SEO is tantamount to placing a brick wall against the front door of a high street shop – you're actually blocking your users from reaching you. You're destined to become part of the noise of the Internet rather than a music maker. You're streaming without a paddle...

So how do you use this book? Dip in and dip out, read it from start to finish – it really doesn't matter. The 52 brilliant ideas contained within are generally quick fixes that should result in immediate benefits to your site, if adopted. If your budget is modest, implementing just a handful of ideas will improve your website rankings and will help you realise your ambitions and the ambitions of your company. Employ all 52 and people really will be throwing themselves down on the floor and proposing – no, wait, I mean finding your website, buying more of your products, reading your information and coming back to your site, again and again.

What's so special about Google then?

Is it really all that?

Google this and Google that! What about Yahoo, AltaVista and all those other search engines? My mum always said 'don't put all your eggs in one basket'...

Say it with numbers

When an Internet user is unable, or unwilling, to guess your URL (Uniform Resource Locator, read website address) they will use a search engine to find you. Now, of all the website visits conducted in the UK and US that were immediately preceded by a search engine search, Google is responsible for the majority. Google is by far the most widely used search engine and the biggest referrer of visitors in the UK (72% of all searches) and the US (62.7% of all searches)[1].

1. Hitwise Search Results (April 2009) *www.hitwise.com*

Google, like Hoover, has achieved a dominance so great, in such a short period of time, that the company name is often used to mean Internet searching. Single execs, looking for companionship, 'google' potential dates before committing to a meal. Parents google a school to decide whether it's suitable for little Frankie's education. Job applicants google the interview staff to learn any interesting snippets that they can bring up at interview (and vice versa). Internet users use Google – a lot.

Google, certainly at the moment, owns the Internet and no matter what our marital status or sexual persuasion it's time for us all to get into bed with Google.

Just flick the switch?

As an e-business adviser and freelance e-consultant I meet a lot of companies with websites. Primarily they all want the same thing – good exposure on Google. But there is no magic switch, there is no instant cure; becoming good bedfellows with Google takes time; you want instant gratification and Google's more interested in pursuing a long-term relationship with you. This may go against everything else we see, hear and feel about the web (overnight success stories, sites plucked from obscurity, servers crashing under the weight of so much traffic...) but that's the deal. Commit seriously to Google and it will commit right back, and when that relationship is forged, it's not just strong, it's *really* strong.

Sleeping with the enemy

Unfortunately, Google doesn't make it easy. You'd think the easiest thing in the world would be for Google to post an FAQ page or a checklist on the site that systematically explained to developers and business owners how to win its favour, but it won't. Why? Well, basically, Google is fed up with people abusing the system and if there's no obvious system, then it's going to make said abuse so much harder. And it works. So, is there an official Google-endorsed guide to Google? No, only unofficial guides, and this is one of them.

Here's an idea for you

Let's see where you are, right now. Type in your domain name on a Google search (less the 'www' and the '.co.uk/.com'). Are you on page 1? 2? 3? Now type in the name of your bestselling product/service/industry. Are you on page 1? 2? 3? OK, now there are plenty of ideas for you to improve that listing and get you not just to the top of the page for each of those searches, but filling page 1 completely, with separate links to areas of your site.

2

I wanna be number 1

Taking the restricted view

No matter which search term I choose, my competitor is always number 1, I'm not even on the first page. How can I compete?

The smaller picture

Whatever industry or service your website offers, it's fair to say that you are part of a very busy marketplace. You're not the first website, nor will you be the last. Understanding, and more importantly accepting, that you are not the only player is a major stepping stone to ensuring that you are successful. I'm serious. No idea is original and deciding to use the web as your sales outlet is certainly not groundbreaking – someone, somewhere has been doing it successfully or unsuccessfully far longer than you, and many more will follow. But don't let that put you off.

Keyword ego

There are top-level keywords in every single industry. As an online toy seller I was obsessed with the keyword 'toys', but it quickly became apparent that I was up against Toys'R'Us and ToyMaster; yet we were in a different market and on long-term marketing spend we simply couldn't compete. The click-throughs we got for paying over the odds for the keyword 'toys' weren't converting into sales. What was the matter? The answer was that we had a specialist offering: traditional-style wooden toys, finger puppets, pram toys and off-the-wall clothing/footwear. The simple fact is that people who typed in the word 'toys' were looking for the latest craze, invariably made out of plastic, which had enjoyed advertising on television. That wasn't the sort of stuff we sold. OK, we sold toys, but not the 'toys' that these people were looking for.

Special and unique

Your potential customers are both of these things – special in that they require extra attention and unique in that they really do think for themselves. We are all guilty of forcing web users into a certain category, but the truth is, they're as different and picky about their web habits as they are about their everyday decisions. Treat them as individuals.

Here's an idea for you

In your opinion, right now, what are the top three keywords that you think are important to your site? Got them? Right, forget about them. They're not important (for now). Now create a list of ten keywords that are the next most important in the list (as far as you're concerned). These are the niche words, the important words, these words will make you rich. Write these words down as we'll use them and turn that process into revenue, I promise.

3

It's not yogurt...

Organic (or natural) versus paid-for

Whatever your views about 'good' bacteria, there is a huge distinction to be made between healthy listings and unhealthy ones.

33% of Internet users perceive a company in the top search engine rankings to be a major brand[1].

Pay for it, you will

I'm not against paid-for listings, not at all. A good AdWords campaign can and will bring profit to a website that exploits this offering well. But before we go down the route of paid-for placement we need to do everything we can to ensure that your site is search-engine friendly and ranking well, without committing to financial outlay – and at the end of the day, AdWords is always going to cost you money, especially in the short term. Have a campaign. But ensure that you are maximising your site to perform well in the natural or organic listings also.

1. iProspect search engine branding survey – **www.iprospect.com**

Your target should be to rank high naturally *and* be featured within the AdWords listings – because two listings on page 1 of Google is always going to look stronger than just a single one.

They're just so switched-on, nowadays

Your average Internet user is getting clever. They are becoming wise to the fact that the search results at the top of the page and on the right-hand side are only there because someone is paying for the privilege. Therefore, many people will actively *not* click through them, and prefer to explore the natural search results – those sites that are there because of their SEO and content merits, not their marketing spend. You must ensure that you are ranking there too.

Here's an idea for you

To get a feel for the disparity and similarities of how websites perform in the paid-for and natural listings make a few searches on Google. Try 'posters', 'auction' and 'toys'. Notice any patterns? Are there some companies you would have thought would be paying for placement who aren't? Now do a specific search for your industry – do you appear on the first page? Who are your competitors? Do they have a good natural listing and/or a paid-for placement? By understanding what others are doing within your market you will quickly ascertain what you need to be doing to compete effectively.

widgets

arch.™

ts

- Thousands of Widgets for Wha

tincidunt arcu. Nullam sodales odio vitae

odo, dui sit amet scelerisque commodo, s

augue.com/ - 12k - Cached - Similar

tium nisi sod

9

4

View askew

How Google sees your site

I wanna become the name everyone thinks of when vacuum cleaners are mentioned... Set realistic goals, strive for them, enjoy the results.

To aspire to be number 1 on Google only exposes the public's general disregard and false understanding that most business owners have for Google, and for search engines in general.

Your major qualifying interest – your cash cows, i.e. your paying customers – aren't the random surfers who type in 'toys' or 'books' or 'flowers'. It's far more specific and targeted than that. Your (and my) customers are after a particular item or service, the long tail if you will, right here, right now. Although branding is very important, if I need a hand-tied bouquet delivered by 10 a.m. tomorrow morning, then I don't care who gets the business, as long as they deliver. And that's true across the board.

View askew – Google's take

Joe Public wants to be number 1 – I do, you do, your competitor does... the list continues. It's quite obvious that we can't all be number 1, so how does it work? Web users are becoming ever more advanced; if they are looking for that hand-tied bouquet, then that's exactly what they will type in as their search terms; they might even add a location. So, if you're a florist in Birmingham, you'd be far better optimising your site to become number 1 for 'bouquet Birmingham', or 'funeral flowers Birmingham' than you would trying to make an impact with the keyword 'flowers'.

Your battle plan

What phrases are your customers using to find you? What phrases *should* be finding you? And what can you do to capitalise on this? The simple answer is to find out what words and phrases Internet users are really using in any given month and capitalising on that information. Google offers you the perfect tool – https://adwords. google.com/select/KeywordToolExternal

Here's an idea for you

Go to the website *https://adwords.google.com/select/KeywordToolExternal* – this is Google's Keyword Tool. Type in the keyword you are interested in tracking. The clever thing about Keyword Tool is that it also returns related results, and thus a single search can return a lot of serious data about the keywords you were interested in exploiting and, often, keywords you weren't. In a matter of minutes you'll be able to see where you're going wrong, what needs to be added to your meta information and your body text and a clear indication of whether you need to be creating multiple sites on the web.

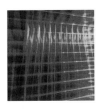 

5

Uncovering the data

Unleashing your inner Miss Marple

Research is critical to any business – what are your competitors doing? What is the market doing? Dust off that magnifying glass, start wearing tweed and let's find out.

Google's Keyword Tool is a great start, but what else can you use to find out more? Well, there is a whole host of sites offering business-critical information about keywords; some you pay for, some you don't. I'm going to concentrate on the paid-for information – because it's strong, accurate and the investment pays for itself many times over with results.

www.wordtracker.com

We might think we know what keywords people often use, and we might think we know how many competitors are out there, but Wordtracker will be able to tell you categorically if that is the case.

Go to the site and enter the keywords or phrases you are interested in. The great thing about Wordtracker is that it will also show you how many users searched for that word today, what the competition is like for your selected keyword or phrase – and give the results a numerical score, known as a KEI, so you will instantly know whether you are one of few or one of many competing for a keyword. If you're lucky there will be some words or phrases with a KEI of more than 300, which means it is a popular keyword with very little competition; any score of more than 50 is well worth optimising. You should focus your marketing attention on these words.

www.nichebot.com

A really handy tool. Nichebot takes its data from both Yahoo! and Wordtracker; it then merges the information and displays the results accordingly. Nichebot uses its own algorithm to display the data, and therefore please note that a good score on Nichebot is a very low number as opposed to the higher the better with Wordtracker.

I think Nichebot is handy if you're short on time, but I've noticed discrepancies between the data provided on Nichebot and the same data you can get from their sources (Yahoo/Wordtracker). Therefore I would run the tests separately if time allowed.

Here's an idea for you

Don't just add these web addresses to your favourites or promise yourself that you'll take a look in a few days – do it, right now. This data is only accurate up to the date of the search. A single look at the data won't allow for peaks and troughs. What you need to be doing is collecting and collating this information, and you should continue to do so over the coming weeks. Create a spreadsheet with the most important keywords and the associated number of searches – are there patterns, trends or fluctuations that might have an impact on your business over a twelve-month period?

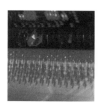

6

Pimp my metadata

The hidden message

**Your message to the search engines is often hidden within the
code that makes up the site – it may be out of sight, but it's
no less important. Here's how to pimp it up.**

Your battle plan

Of all the information you can include in the header of your site,
your title is by far the one that's most appreciated and regarded by
Google. This dictates the bit of text that appears right at the top of
the page of your own or your user's web browser, and it's
confirmation that they've arrived at the correct destination and
your site has what they want. For example, if I had a site selling
rare stamps I'd want the title to reflect something along the lines
of 'rare and hard-to-find stamps, for serious collectors – 24-hour
delivery'.

Meta keywords

Your keywords are the words that you feel your website should be ranked under. For instance, if you sell skateboards and related products, your homepage keywords are going to want to include the words skaters will be interested in –

```
<META name="keywords" content="skate shoes,
footwear, skateboarding, heelys, skateboards,
inline skates, skate clothing, hoodys,
t-shirts, tees, jeans">
```

But the classic problem, which most websites have, is coming up with a great list of keywords and then repeating them on every single page. No! Keep it specific. Only use a keyword (or for that matter a reference in your title or description) if the word is used in the page within the body text – if not, you'll be penalised.

My developer said that Google doesn't pay any attention to keywords any more – and they'd be right, they don't. But although this is about Google, I'm not blinkered enough to ignore the other search engines out there that do pay attention to meta keywords – in fact, that's a whopping 20% of the search market, constituting one in five of your potential traffic. Not to be sniffed at or ignored. Put it like this, the day Amazon stops using meta keywords is the day I'll stop; these people spend millions researching the web.

Meta description

So someone does a Google search and they're presented with about twelve results per page. They see a long list of web addresses and a bit of introductory text about the site... where do you think that text comes from? Well, if you don't include a meta description it will be randomly chosen from a page on your site, and, quite frankly, might not make an awful lot of sense. Alternatively, you can add a meta description, which is a short, one- or two-sentence description of your website. This should also be a sales message to potential visitors – so what's going to make them click on your link and not a competitor's? Strong, clean copy is the answer: a sales message, a teaser, a call to action to encourage them through to you.

Here's an idea for you

Write a one-sentence descriptive comment that describes what information and products users will find on your homepage. This will become your title. Once you're happy with that, personalise it a little bit and the result will become your meta description, but don't stop there. You've only answered the problem of the homepage, now you need to repeat the process for every single page on your site. Remember less is more and be specific.

7

That keyword is so owned

Satellite sites

If you have an engineering website and the company name is ABC Ltd, is your best course of action to rely upon *www.abcltd.co.uk?* Well, no, not really.

Guerrilla marketing

With the best will in the world, calling your website by your company name may seem the most normal and natural course of action... and it's certainly worth buying the domain name just to protect yourself. However, to truly sell and market yourself through the Internet you need to understand how web users operate and how they are likely to find you.

I spend my days advising website owners how best to improve their sites and how to get them noticed. This week, for example, I met with a client who offers training courses to managers of businesses, based in

Hampshire. He'd been operating using a website domain name similar to www.abcltd.co.uk, which was fine, but was doing him no favours in terms of attracting new customers unfamiliar with his company. A quick search on the web (I use www.123-reg.co.uk) revealed that at the time of writing the following domain names were available:

www.leadership-management-training.net –
available from £18 for 2 years
www.management-training.gb.com – available from £30 for 2 years
www.management-training-hampshire.co.uk –
available from £6 for 2 years
www.management-training-hampshire.com –
available from £18 for 2 years
www.management-skills-training.co.uk – available from £6 for 2 years
www.business-management-training.net –
available from £18 for 2 years

All keyword heavy, available and cheap!

Case study

I had a website called www.toytopia.co.uk (query Google, even now, and it's flooded with references to a company that ceased trading four years ago). Whilst the Toytopia site did very well in terms of traffic and customers, we noticed that some of the items we sold were being featured on the TV and in the Sunday supplements. This was nothing to do with us, but we were obviously selling items that really appealed and we wanted to capitalise on this free PR. A quick search of our bestsellers revealed that wheeliebugs were a major cash cow for us and within weeks we launched www.wheeliebugs.co.uk which was a dedicated site specifically for wheeliebugs. This product was being featured in a magazine or a news item every week; all we did was provide a sales outlet based on the keywords that people would remember – in this case, the actual name of the product, 'wheeliebugs'. Although the Toytopia site ranked highly on a wheeliebugs search, nothing is stronger than owning the very domain name itself – the keywords that encapsulate the product or the theme. The site rocked and became a business in its own right. It cost us £3.00 for the domain name for 12 months and £200 to transfer aspects of the site across, and netted almost £140,000.

A word of warning

If you buy keyword-heavy domains, be sure to set up small (even single page) websites at each address, rather than opting for the simple re-direct option – Google really doesn't like this and may unleash the fury. It's better to have a keyword-heavy site (albeit one page) with a link through to your main site than to force users across using a re-direct. Theoretically, if you get your SEO right, you'll have a couple of listings on page one of Google's search results made up of the main site and the satellite sites, thus forcing your competitor's sites further and further down the listings.

Here's an idea for you

Using a variety of search tools, find out what keywords are being used and the number of people searching in any given month or day. Does this sort of traffic seem attractive? Would 1% or 2% of those people make a huge difference to your business? If so, it's time to start setting up satellite websites to capture as much search traffic as possible.

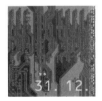

8

Analyse this

Google Analytics

Without knowing how you're performing now, you've no way of knowing if any of your changes make a blind bit of difference.

The sign up

Google Analytics is a popular service. So popular, in fact, it can take a few weeks for you to be approved after signing up. Bear this in mind and start the sign-up process as soon as you can. Once you are approved, you will be issued with a small bit of code, which will need to be added to every page of your site that you want to track – for most of us, this means every page. Your user name and password will allow you access to a whole host of statistics regarding your site.

In a nutshell

So, what's it all about? Well, Analytics is a great way to check visually what's going on in terms of traffic on your site – how many people are visiting, what they're looking at, how long they stay and the city or town from where they are visiting you. Not bad, for free. With the data you are then able to set targets and goals for the performance of the site, and this data is collected and presented to you through an easy to use graphical interface. If you are using, or plan to use, paid-for adverts through Google (AdWords) then it makes sense to sign up as the two programs are so interrelated and in a way interdependent.

Other benefits?

Again, Google make no mention of it, but I can't help feeling that having some Google code on your site is a pretty good indication of how important you feel Google is to your site. Therefore, I can't help feeling that – unofficially – your loyalty and acceptance of Google does not go unnoticed and unrewarded in terms of how often your site is visited by the Googlebot, and subsequently ranked...

Its word is law...

Actually it's not, and at the end of the day Google is a business looking to make profit, so, whilst at the moment the Analytics program works really well it should always be used in conjunction with your own stats package (usually standard with most websites now). It is interesting to compare and contrast the data from both sources – they should, of course, be telling you the same thing, but that is not always the case.

Here's an idea for you

Pop over to *www.google.com/analytics* and sign up. Once you receive approval add (or have your developer add) the 'urchin' code to your web pages, and within 24 hours you'll be receiving accurate data about activity on your site. (Repeat the process for each and every domain name/site you own.) You can track as many separate domains through one Analytics account as you wish.

9

Destination me

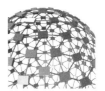

The importance of in-bound links

Once it worked like this: I've got a website, you've got a website, let's reciprocally link. Now this won't help either of you. The rules have most definitely changed!

In-bound is king

People abused the system and now we're all being punished. I should no longer mention a friend's or a favoured business contact's website on my site unless it has a direct relevance to the content of my own site. Gone are the days where you'd click on a 'links' page and see a cornucopia of interesting, sassy and amusing sites – why? Well, if a site is still playing this game, it is likely to be penalised. Therefore it's in the site owner's best interest to remove all links that don't positively affect his or her own rankings. That means getting rid of the chaff and actively seeking and encouraging the great and the good. So, who are the good?

PageRank

There is some slight confusion over this name. Whilst, in effect, it means the rank of your web page or website, the actual name derives from Larry Page, one of Google's founders. He created an algorithm to assign a numerical value to a website or page – essentially designed to promote relevance, authority and clear meaning. This numerical value (expressed as a figure between 0 and 10) reflects the popularity of a website and its 'usefulness', which incorporates a number of defining factors, but let's concentrate on the relevance of links here.

What about out-bound?

This certainly shouldn't be your focus, but there's concentrating on making your site search-engine friendly and there's offering your users something value-added and providing a service. If you are selling a product and feel that adding a link to the manufacturer or a fan site or any other site will benefit your own, then your quest to make your site search-engine friendly shouldn't become a neurotic obsession. Include the link; your primary customer is your human user, not the Googlebot. Remaining search-engine friendly is, of course, important – but if you can enrich the life of your user, and help them feel comfortable with the information you provide, they're more likely to buy your product or service, or link to you. This is what will make your website a success, not Google.

Here's an idea for you

Download the Google Toolbar from *www.google.com/tools/firefox/toolbar* and if you're not using Firefox as your web browser, simply type 'Google Toolbar' into Google. It will then reply with the correct URL depending on your browser. Google's Toolbar will offer you a number of tools, but most importantly will display the PageRank of any given page you are visiting. Examples of sites with a high PageRank are *www.bbc.co.uk* and *www.google.co.uk* (no surprise there!). For a hardcore explanation into the mathematics and algorithm behind Google's PageRank check out this listing on Wikipedia: *http://en.wikipedia.org/wiki/PageRank*

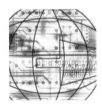 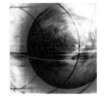

Who's lookin'?

Keyword bias

Research suggests that only 7% of websites employ any search engine optimisation whatsoever. Get this right and you're on your way to fame and fortune...

Finding key phrases to attract potential customers is critical. Most businesses that decide to trade on the Internet establish themselves first offline. They have created a brand and they try to replicate that brand online. But their brand is non-transferable, as is. You have to work on building both an offline and an online presence.

Far too specific, or not...

If you ask Marlene, who owns the domain name www.marlenescakes.co.uk, where she ranks on Google, the chances are she'll say number 1. But she'll be referring to searches conducted containing the keywords 'marlene' and 'cakes' – and this is not how people search. No one knows Marlene, so, in need of some cake, they will search for 'cake' or 'wedding cake' or 'birthday cake, Manchester', etc. Marlene and her site do not exist, as far as the search engines are concerned, because she hasn't optimised her site to this level. Users will be directed to the sites that have capitalised on the generic search terms (or keywords) and the site that appears in the search results will gain the customer, even though, theoretically, they might be on the other side of the world. Marlene may well have the most appropriate offering, but if users can't find her, the site may as well not be there.

Finding the most appropriate key phrases

It's all very well having a sexy business name such as 'Orion Services' but the name itself means nothing. Are you a scientific agency dealing with the mapping of the stars, a washing-machine repairer or a business consultancy? Who knows? Your potential customer certainly doesn't know, and no amount of searching on Google is likely to find you. Your domain name should incorporate your key deliverables. If you're a guest house on the Isle of Lewis, then include some of those terms in your domain name. I used to sell wooden toys online and the business was called Toytopia – a clever name simply because it incorporated the keyword that defined the product. If you provide management training it's no good calling yourself Atlantis Ltd; far better to be Management-Trainer.co.uk. These are the sort of phrases that UK Internet users employ, so work it to your advantage.

Here's an idea for you

Within your web browser, open your website and view its source code to see your own meta keywords (in some versions of Internet Explorer, for example, you do this by clicking on 'view' and then 'source'). Use the same technique to view your competitors' pages and those of any other websites that interest you. Chances are you'll soon learn what works, and what doesn't. You'll see what techniques your competitors are employing and what can be copied across to your site – and all this critical information is available for free!

11

Who are ya?

It's all in the detail, so does your Nominet record tally?

Is what you say about yourself true? Is it still the case? People (and Google) can check – so what does your WHOIS record say about you?

Inadvertent mistake

When many of us set up a website, the idea – or even the company – is still to be fully created. This is normal and not a problem. When you are buying the domain name (or instructing others to buy on your behalf) you, personally, quote your home address as the contact. You register yourself as 'non-trading' because, right now, you're not.

However, over time the business is launched and the WHOIS details remain the same – you might be employing fifteen staff and turning over a couple of million, but your WHOIS record implies that you are a one man band operating out of a garage. Most users won't notice, but some might – especially customers who might want to do business with you, such as running a joint venture, a co-promotion or even becoming a buyer of your business. And, more importantly, Google can see. Again, there's no specific mention, but if you're running a .com business from the UK (or conversely a .co.uk business from outside of the UK) this shows up in terms of where the server is hosted, the physical contact address you've quoted and the contact email address. Keep it local for the market you want to appeal to.

You can run a WHOIS report from numerous websites. For starters, try **www.whois.net** and check everything is present and correct. If your website developers have accidentally put their address as the registrant, then have this changed. For .co.uk addresses contact Nominet at **www.nominet.org.uk**

Staying in control

Although your service provider will probably email you many months in advance of your domain name expiring, what if they forget? Or go out of business? Or deliberately don't tell you because another one of their clients is interested in the domain? It's your responsibility to re-register your domain names, not anyone else's. Use WHOIS to determine when the expiration date is and then set a reminder in your diary or online calendar one month beforehand so you can check it has been taken care of. There's nothing harder than trying to get hold of a domain that has expired – in fact, it's far easier for a complete stranger to come along and buy it from under your nose.

Here's an idea for you

Make sure your WHOIS information reflects you and your business in the best possible light. There's nothing wrong with working from home (I do it too) but make the first line of the address look like a business: 'Company House, 14 Wilton Road...' Yes, it's nonsense, but it works and if I was interested in talking to you at a commercial level, I'd have a very different view of a business that has its own premises than one apparently trading from a residential address. As far as Google is concerned, a UK address for a .co.uk domain name is always going to look more legitimate than a foreign one or a PO Box number.

12

Open with a joke

Keyword prominence and relevance

Google, for all its head-of-the-table bravado, just likes a snappy, sassy introduction to a website – no idealistic diatribe, just the truth in bite-sized pieces...

Less is more, baby...

Although there are some complicated algorithms at play (which are constantly altering) the guideline to a page that will work successfully on Google is a page that is created simply and follows this basic premise. When you (or your developer) are creating a web page, the top 25% of the page and the very bottom of the page are the most important. This is not to say that everything in between is ignored, far from it – but what Google wants to see is prominence given to the critical or key words and phrases by which you are looking to be ranked.

Don't, therefore, waste the prime real estate or the top of a page with a lengthy introduction to the site or the topic but get right in there – go straight for the jugular, and be conscious of the prominence and relevance you give to the keywords being quoted. If you sell trendy T-shirts then you need to be dropping in the brands that you carry, not a monologue about the importance of T-shirts or a history of the garment. Start selling product, both to the user and to Google. Let them all know that you mean business.

Equally, the very bottom of the page is important. Does your page taper off with a couple of half-hearted links to the privacy policy and a © statement? Or does it include the pertinent navigational options repeated as text-only links that will add both to the user's ability to continue navigating your site and to Google's ability to notice yet another reference to a certain type of T-shirt, thus helping you to rise up the rankings because of relevance and prominence?

H tags

The jury's out as to their weighting, but I remain convinced that as long as you don't try to abuse the system (by tagging every subject as H1) then, considering all other factors, they work. H tags are the way you tell the search engines that this 'H' (or header), is worth paying attention to – **it's like making a sentence bold**; it gets noticed. Whilst you may have physically altered the text to be bold or italic or presented in a larger point size, Google ignores this as it's cosmetic. It's looking for H tags, and your job is to list them in order of relevance.

If there are four main focuses to your web page then you're well within your rights to label each one with an H tag, ideally listed in ranking order – H1, H2, H3 and so on. Though labelling each topic with H1 might win you a short-term gain, it's foolhardy and will eventually be penalised. Equally, if there's only one major topic or point to the page, add your H1 tag, but don't be tempted to add others for the sake of it.

Here's an idea for you

If you are yet to employ H tags, then reassess your web pages and assign them to the pertinent points on each page. If you are already using H tags, check that they are being utilised correctly. Are they relevant? Do they add to the site? Will they help or hinder the site being ranked? If there are any more than six on a page, ditch the overkill.

13

Laid-back surfers

The Google search

Google has made us all lazy: you want to find a site, you search. You want to find something on a particular website, you search – so do you offer search?

Seek and ye shall find

When users first visit a website they've no idea whether there are ten pages or ten thousand pages behind the site – and sometimes, in our cash-rich, time-poor lifestyles, we haven't even got a few seconds to spare to find out. You might have spent hours agonising over the clever navigation and categories that define your site; it might actually be quite good. But there are navigators and there are searchers, and behavioural profiling would suggest that the latter are becoming the norm. Therefore, if users visit your site after following a link from Google they will want instant gratification – the answer on a plate. Can you offer them what it is they want and need? It's all very well for you to know that within three clicks they can explore the depth and breadth of your entire product catalogue, but that's a massive twenty seconds of time and thought – which many web users will not spare you. A search tool is the answer, and is something you should give high priority to implementing.

In bed with Google, again...

It's that old way of thinking, yet again, but common sense will tell you that if you can't afford to install an integrated search tool on your own site, then the Google Search has to be the only alternative. They are not going to ignore or punish a site that has included Google code within the HTML – this is mutual back-rubbing at its best. Offer your users a chance to search your site; they'll love you for it. You can download Enterprise Solutions from ***www.google.com/enterprise/enterprise_search.html***

Here's an idea for you

Visit all of your competitor's sites and pay particular attention to their search tool, or if they don't have one, note that down. Now, what do you like about their search and what doesn't work? Search for both obvious industry-specific terms and the more obscure ones. What's coming back – helpful, pertinent results? Nothing? Irrelevant results? Or worse, the wrong results? Armed with the knowledge of where they are going wrong, it's time to invest in your own search tool, or to use Google's. Despite its flaws it will prove very useful in the short term while you are busy creating your own.

14

Selling out

Accepting Google advertising

It may be that over 90% of your visitors don't order or contact you... so you may as well try and make some money out of them another way.

Losing customers

Yes, the price you pay for offering any form of linked advertising on your site is that you are effectively sending traffic away from your site – but you are getting paid for it. If your site is a portal or an information site, then advertising will be one of your major revenue streams.

Google vs. specific advertisers

The problem for most small or newer sites is that they don't have a huge amount of traffic, and established advertisers aren't going to want to work with them until they can prove big numbers. Google isn't fussy, it will work with everyone and anyone. If you want to start earning money from your site immediately join the

AdSense programme. Again, there's no proof of this on the Google site, but another bit of Google code on your site must make the Googlebot more favourable to your site – expect more visits and a higher ranking.

Make money from your site

It's true: at 2 a.m. someone, somewhere might be interested in buying something. That someone might be looking for the very thing that you sell via an affiliate. That item might be a book that retails at £10.99, and your commission might be 10%. You might argue, is it worth it for £1.09? Well, as a single sale, probably not. But what if you have a targeted audience visiting your site and buying products via your affiliate deals? Suddenly that £1.09 is repeated again and again and becomes more, and more, and more. To sign up to AdSense, go to

https://www.google.com/adsense/login/en_GB/?hl=en_GB

I would only really consider this option if you have a significant amount of traffic to make this process worthwhile. The financial reward must compensate for the dilution of your own brand/site and the fact that you are sending potential customers away.

Here's an idea for you

Join AdSense and, once your account has been created, add a link on a page of your site. Not on your homepage but maybe on a page that is not part of your core offering, or one that just needs a bit more content that you haven't got round to writing yet. See if AdSense works for you. Are customers clicking on it? Are the revenues pretty good? Would they be even more if you added the campaign across the entire site? Give it a go and see what happens.

15

Say that again?

Keyword proximity

The art of good text on a website is not flowery prose and poetic sentiment – it's all about shouting about what's on offer.

This means what the user (and Google) can find on your page and answering the very basic question: do you sell/provide the information or product that I am looking for? If you can answer this in your first paragraph you're well on your way to a successful site.

Writing like a pro

It's all very well having world-beating content on your site, but is it in the right place? Web pages can be very long, sometimes this is good and sometimes this is bad, but don't be too concerned with length of text. Instead focus your attention on where on the page the keywords and phrases that you've spent so long researching are being utilised in the most effective way possible.

We've seen that Google favours keywords and phrases appearing right at the top of the page, and therein lies the key. This isn't a novel or a play that you're writing; we don't need a gentle fluffy introduction to what's going on, we don't need to be warmed up. You need to come out with all guns blazing, with a definitive statement that summarises what is contained on that page. It should be rich in keywords and phrases, direct, clear and constantly calling the user to action. Use the rest of the text to explain and qualify your statements. Not the other way round.

Good 'spider food'

Although it is the human user you must ultimately appeal to if the website itself is going to be effective, the Googlebot and other search engine spiders must also be at the forefront of your mind when creating copy for your web pages. This all boils down to a neat little marriage that will keep both parties interested and happy, and this is known as keyword density. If you flood your text with keywords it won't make sense to your end users and will mean that they abandon the site. Therefore you should be looking for a density of about 4%, which means for every one hundred words of text on your page, you should mention your keyword four times. Stick with this rule and the spiders, the bots, the crawlers and even the human users will regard your content as strong.

Here's an idea for you

Pick a product page or a page that describes one of your services and take a long hard look at the text. Have you mentioned everything, at least once, that was hinted at in the metadata? Have you placed the most important keywords and phrases (including brands) within the first and second paragraphs of text? Can the user/Google click on some or all of these keywords to learn more? If not, start reworking the text so that it appeals to both the human user and to Google. Yes, you will need to compromise, but this is business, not a creative writing course.

16

Jargon busting

Hits, visitors, page views and uniques...

As with all industries the world of websites is peppered with its own lingo. Get to know it well and nobody will be able to pull the wool over your avatar.

Hits

The most abused and wrongly used statistic referring to web activity. You've heard people say 'I get 100,000 hits a month!' Meaningless. A hit refers to each file sent by the server to a web browser – therefore, if you have a page that contains seven images, chances are those images plus the HTML file supporting them will register as eight hits. The numbers get quickly out of hand and you've no real idea how many visitors your site is getting.

Page views

A more accurate measurable, because the figure disregards how many hits or files make up the web page. It simply measures how many times a web page was served up. The problem with page views is that you don't know whether it was one user looking at twenty pages or twenty visitors looking at one page each...

Visitors/uniques

This should be the number that you are paying most attention to. This is the truest representation of how popular your site is. More accurate than hits or page views, your visitor numbers show how many people actually came to your site.

PPC

Price Per Click is the financial reward someone will pay you for every click they receive from an advert placed on your site – or the price you pay Google, for example, every time someone clicks on your AdWords advert. Clients often ask what a good PPC rate is and the answer is that it depends. It's only worth what someone is prepared to pay.

CPM

This is less and less common nowadays but some advertisers don't want to be messing around with a micro-payment for every single click-through. They're looking at this relationship in the macro sense and expect you to be sending over shedloads of visitors. They therefore prefer to work in terms of thousands of visitors rather than anything smaller. The letter M is the Latin representation of 1000, and thus PPM is the Cost Per Thousand.

Here's an idea for you

I'm assuming that you've already signed up to Google Analytics and the information is flooding through, but don't just rely on these statistics, get a second opinion. Now, maybe your developer has bolted on a website statistics function to your site, but if not check out ***www.opentracker.com***, which is a great tool for measuring activity and, if you're considering marketing your site on search engines other than Google, essential.

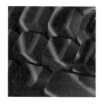

17

Here, look over here

Registering with search engines

Google and the other search engines are good – but they're not omnipotent. Let them know you've arrived on the scene; be bold, be noticed and be listed.

Lost in the noise

There are literally millions of new websites and web pages being added to the Internet every day. Google is trying to keep up, but likes us to flag a major change or a new development. Launching a site and just expecting to be found by search engines and customers alike is just not going to work. You need to leave a trail of breadcrumbs and, better yet, set off an unmistakable fanfare to announce your arrival. Manually submit your web address to the major search engines to get the ball rolling...

Google
http://www.google.com/addurl

Or, if you're feeling lazy, type 'Add URL' into Google and you'll see the link you need. Google offers a whole host of Webmaster tools which are worth investigating, but for now fill in the blanks and submit. Expect a visit from the Googlebot within about three weeks.

Yahoo!
http://search.yahoo.com/info/submit.html

Not as slick as the Google web address, and you have to register with Yahoo! to utilise the page, but it's worth it and recommended.

AltaVista
http://addurl.altavista.com/addurl/default

Lycos
www.lycos.co.uk/inc/foot/addasite.html

If you fancy jump-starting your appearance on any other search engines just search for 'submit URL' on your search engine of choice. Be sure that you only submit yourself once in any given month as the search engines see repeated listing requests as spam, so check whether your developer has done it first. Have one member of staff responsible for submitting to all the engines.

Paying the hired help

Avoid the many hundreds of sites that offer to submit your site to all the major search engines on your behalf – they want money from you for what is a really simple exercise. Also, you can't be sure it's been done and you won't know if they've done it correctly. Lastly, most of the submission pages ask you to copy the wavy security text they provide so that they can determine whether the submit URL request has been generated by a human user or software – you can bet your bottom server that they will pay more attention to those requests generated by hand.

Here's an idea for you

Once you've submitted your site to all the major search engines, put a note in your diary for three months' time. Unless you're noticing that the search engines are visiting regularly, you're going to need to remind them to come again and check out what's new. This isn't spamming, it's just common sense. Keep this up for about a year, by which time you'll see that they visit on a regular basis.

18

Essential code?

Meta robots, etc...

Talking to robots – your little friends out there in cyberspace – may not be as mad as it seems. But take care, not every robot out there wants to be your mate...

Meta robots

Google pays little attention to your meta keywords but, that said, it's still worth including them if for no better reason than helping you plan out the content of your web pages. I've come across some websites that seem to have an entire constitution and manifesto set up for visiting robots – but if those website owners understood how Google operated a little better, it would quickly become apparent that a lot of these commands and instructions are pretty redundant. They're better off removed.

When the Googlebot lands on a page of your site it wants to index that page and then use the links to find out what happens next. So, if you notice the command 'robots, follow' in your code, get rid of it; you're just slowing the Googlebot down and confusing your message. The Googlebot was going to follow whether you invited it to do so or not.

No index/no follow

There might be a reason that you don't want Google to concentrate its efforts on certain pages because they are (content-wise) inferior to other pages on your site. If this is the case, then it is a good idea to employ 'noindex' or 'nofollow' and allow the Googlebot to get to the money pages quickly and without hindrance.

Meta revisit-after

Get rid of it – who are you to tell Google when they should pay you a visit? The Googlebot will visit when it damn well pleases and you should be grateful it does. Just make sure that there's something new for Google to index every time it visits, be it a new image, some text or a new page.

Caution

Some robots are written not to scan or index your site, but are simply unleashed on the web to cause you annoyance by clogging up the server, demanding too many pages too quickly or generally making a nuisance of themselves. This may well happen to your site, but I wouldn't advise blocking access to robots just because of the threat of malicious activity. The benefits of being open and available to the Googlebot and all the other search engine spiders far outweighs the possibility of a denial of service attack.

Here's an idea for you

Start reading your server log files and actually try to make some sense of them. Look out for named robots such as Googlebot or WebCrawler and see what happened when they visited. What pages were accessed? How long did the robot spend on the site? Most importantly, what pages were not accessed? This will show you if there are any holes in your navigation and site map, and allow you to rationalise the site to be both user- and robot-friendly.

19

Me in France no. 113

Using images correctly

No matter how pretty a picture, Google can't see it. It can only see the image's filename and if that says something like 'logo.jpg' you've got your work cut out...

Toytopia case study

If you run an e-commerce store you need to pay more attention than most as to how images are named. Ensure that every image is named to promote the site and the product to Google rather than just offering a random alphanumeric filename. At Toytopia we had a lot of success with wheeliebugs and we carried five different types, each available in two different sizes. Rather than naming them 'wheelie1.jpg' through to 'wheelie10.jpg' part of the success of the site was due in part to the naming of files. For example, we used 'wheeliebug-ride-on-toy-mouse-large.jpg'.

Not only is this Google-friendly, it made it a lot easier for me to find a specific image within the images folder. When you are carrying hundreds if not thousands of products, you'll be pleased you spent a few extra seconds naming each image file correctly. Remember the text that makes up the image name is adding to the keywords being found on the page. You've mentioned the product a couple of times in your copy, there's a navigational link and it's reinforced within the filename of the image – Google's beginning to get all dewy-eyed about your site and that means a good positioning on the search results.

Again, taking the example above, 'logo.jpg' is not doing you any favours. Reinforce your brand, your product/s, your purpose with something like this: 'Toytopia_online_wooden_toys_logo.jpg'.

Oh! Big boy...

If you're responsible for uploading images to your site be aware of the resolution. If you want to print a digital image then high-res is critical, but for the web 72 dots per inch (DPI) is all you require. Any more is wasted information that computer monitors can't process – big images slow down sites and annoy users. Most image editing software now offers a tool to alter the resolution of an image. Use it.

Here's an idea for you

If you run a site where a number of members of staff are adding content, it's time to write a policy or house rules document outlining the procedure for doing this. Even if you're a one man band, this is still an important exercise, as it will allow you to check all of the existing content and ensure it's optimised for Google. House style can be as simple as ensuring that paragraphs of text are broken up with the paragraph (<P>) command rather than a break (<BR>), right up to a detailed guide on how to name images, use H tags and ensure good keyword proximity at the top of the copy rather than the bottom.

20

Don't cloak, just kiss

Being upfront with your intentions

No matter how good your lipstick and foundation, Google can see through your thinly veiled disguise – far better to try to look good naked.

Seen it all before...

Google is like the ageing history teacher you had at your secondary school – coming across all cool and friendly, but if you push the boundaries too much you'll get a board rubber thrown at your head. If you (or your SEO contractor) think you've come up with a great way to trick Google, think again. It's been done, it's been spotted and anyone else who tries it will be penalised. Google hates cheats and the penalties can be severe.

Google means business

The highest-profile case of Google throwing its toys out of the pram has to be the German BMW site in early 2006. BMW.de had created a load of keyword-heavy 'doorway' pages that were only visible to the Googlebot; human users would be redirected to a different page. Now this goes against Google's rules:

> 'If an SEO creates deceptive or misleading content on your behalf, such as doorway pages or "throwaway" domains, your site could be removed entirely from Google's index.'

Google's response? Well BMW.de was effectively removed from the Google index; they no longer existed as far as searchers were concerned. They were given a PageRank of 0, no cached versions of pages could be found and there was no mention of BMW.de anywhere within Google. Pretty harsh.

Cloaked content

Whilst you may well have a legitimate reason for having hidden content on your site, if you can avoid it, do. The Googlebot is pretty busy; all those billions of web pages to index and not enough hours in the day. The reality is that Google is not going to ask you questions about your intentions, it's just going to make a decision on the evidence presented. Most websites use hidden content for nefarious reasons and you'll be tarred with the same brush. At best, that page will suffer; at worst, the entire site will be penalised. If you're unsure, don't.

Here's an idea for you

Whether you built the site yourself or employed a developer, take the time out to look through the code and pay particular attention to any colour commands especially relating to text. Your developer might have thought they were doing you a favour by embedding loads of keywords at the bottom of the page in the same colour as the background... but Google's just waiting to smack some naughty bottoms.

21

Content is king

Building pages the right way round

Writing good web copy is hard, but the time you spend perfecting your offering will result in a more successful website.

Every page should be...

There are always exceptions to every rule, but as a rule of thumb aim for at least 250–300 words per page. Any less than this and you're going to struggle with effective keyword density and run the risk of 'spamming' the page with a long list of keywords that won't make sense to human users.

Support the text with images. This will help break up the page for users and also offers you a chance to drop keywords into the HTML through the naming of the images.

Update your web pages regularly. Add content whenever and wherever you can. This can be alterations or additions to the body copy or the inclusion of downloadable files such as PDF or Word documents – but note that Google won't index the copy within these files, so make sure the best stuff is on the website itself.

Get your users to add to your content. Offer them the chance to review products or post on a forum as this will do wonders for your site. If Google sees new content every time it pays a visit, you'll be rewarded with a higher ranking.

One phrase per page

If it's possible on your site, you'll want to create a separate and distinct page for every keyword you are interested in capturing. For example, if you have settled on fifteen phrases then you'll need at least fifteen pages, and each one should be optimised for that one phrase using the density rule of about 4%. By optimising each page for one keyword or phrase you are giving Google a clear indication that each page has a clear and distinct message. That results in individual pages enjoying their own rank on the Google search.

Here's an idea for you

Don't look at your website and think 'I need to rewrite this entire site'. Start small and the task will be manageable, so choose your bestselling product or service and begin with that page. Remember keyword density and proximity, and the symbiotic relationship between your metadata and your body copy. Fix that page and then pick another.

22

Whose page? My page!

Owning page 1

It's all very well being number 1 on Google, but don't sell yourself short – next stop: being number 1, 2, 3, 4, 5, 6, 7, 8, 9, 10... Here's how.

Stacking the cards in your favour

It's important to buy and/or create keyword-heavy satellite websites to capitalise on what words and phrases users really type into a Google search. Let's say, for argument's sake, you've now bought and built seven domains that have all been optimised for their specific target keywords. Now, on top of this, you've been applying many other ideas to your main website and three individual web pages relating to that keyword have been noticed and ranked highly by Google. Great! So what happens next?

You'll have realised by now that your homepage is not necessarily the most relevant page for every visitor and, assuming you've been optimising, there are specific pages on your site being returned by Google. This is the first step towards you taking over the world. You see, what you really want to be aiming for is not just to be number 1 on a Google search, but to *own* page one: every reference, all ten natural/organic spaces and – in an ideal world – all of the sponsored listings.

Between the seven satellite sites you've got operating and the three specific web pages being returned when a user types in a phrase, the net result is that on the surface it appears that the user is being offered a variety of ten separate and independent websites. The truth of the matter is that you are behind all of them – it doesn't matter which one they decide to click on; you've got them in your clutches. And your competitors? Well, as you know yourself, if you're not on page 1, you're not in the running…

Resting on your laurels

To achieve seven or eight listings on page 1 of Google is not easy; in fact, the more competitive your industry the harder it is. Website optimisation tends to become a game between a few websites all trying to outdo each other and curry Google's favour. You will see some movement in your rankings (both up and down) as you tweak, and as your competitors tweak their sites. This is why resting on your laurels is impossible. SEO has to be an addictive habit, you need to return to it again and again or someone else is going to knock you off the top spot. Having a number of sites to play with means more work, but you'll have an unfair advantage over your competitors.

Here's an idea for you

If you run an e-commerce store, consider the possibility of launching a new site selling exactly the same products as you do now, but under a different keyword-heavy domain name and on which the products cost at least 10–20% more than they do on your existing site. You may well be incredibly surprised by your increased revenue (for minimal investment) – and that's two of the ten spots taken up on the Google results page...

23

Face/off

Posing as two different brands

Alter egos, they say, are a sign of madness. But in the wacky world of e-commerce, you'd be mad not to talk to yourself.

Open your mind

One of the most influential people I met during my ongoing tenure within the Internet industry (who has asked to remain nameless) was an unassuming chap who approached me after I was speaking at a networking event. At the time my online toy business was doing very well for itself and things were good. I explained my business, its successes, its problems and generally how everything was going. I was expecting some sort of congratulations or sycophantic praise and instead he said, 'Well, if it works on that one domain, why not launch the same business under a different brand, again and again?' Confused, I asked him to explain and now have pleasure in paraphrasing his response.

Dr Jekyll and Mr Hyde

If you've proven the business model, your website works and you've got a loyal customer base, so why settle for one website? Yes, there's a cost involved in redesigning sites, hosting fees and the setting up of new companies – but, in the grand scheme of things, considering that all of the content/products/reviews/knowledge is already collected and documented – how hard would it be to re-invent yourself as your own competitor? I know it sounds a bit daft, but think about it: you're always going to have to share page 1 of the Google search results with somebody, so why not make it your alter ego?

Am I Pat or Patricia?

Here's the deal. You've got a website and a product/service that works. Launch it again, only alter the pricing structure – you can go higher or lower (I would try the former first!). A new brand, a new-look site, a new SEO campaign and possibly a new AdWords campaign: in effect, two completely different websites selling similar products. Lo and behold, you're both competing for the top spot on Google for certain keywords – not a problem – and you've forced a competitor onto page 2... It doesn't really matter whether the user decides to click on and buy from website number 1 or number 2; they're both you under different names.

Thinking that I'd successfully mastered this man's advice I launched another website selling exactly the same toys for 10% more. It worked, really well in fact, and I wrote to thank him for his advice. He replied: 'Never mind one extra site, launch 200 sites all selling the same thing – own the product, don't just sell it…'.

Here's an idea for you

Dig out the calculator and start working out what it will cost you to launch your site all over again, under a different brand. Work out how much you want to increase or decrease your pricing structure and, budget allowing, go for it. If that site works, try another, and another, and another…

24

How y'doin'?

Benchmarking your SEO performance

So, you think your site's performing pretty well on the search engines? Fancy taking a closer look?

www.marketleap.com

Marketleap offers a whole heap of advice on SEO and search marketing and it's really worth taking time out to read the information. They also offer three powerful tools which are well worth having a play with – and yes, they're free. Let's take a closer look at Link Popularity and Keyword Verification.

Link Popularity

So you've written off to all of these websites and requested an in-bound (or backwards) link; you might have even received a response to say you're being added. Well, it's time to check. Click on Link Popularity on the Marketleap site and enter your URL, and you'll be able to see how many websites link to you and – the best bit – who they are.

Now run the same tool but test your competitor's site: who's linking to that site? It's those websites you need to target as they're already proven to be link givers, and I'm guessing they're all pretty relevant to your product/service or industry. Thanks for all the hard work, competitor! You can also use *www.linkpopularity.com* for a similar service.

Keyword Verification

Again, all you need to do is enter your URL and Marketleap does all the hard work. This tool allows you to check quickly whether your site can be found on the major search engines in relation to the keyword or phrase you are querying. If you're not ranked within the first three pages, then Marketleap counts this as not ranked – because beyond page 3, your site is as good as invisible to users. What you're looking for is a row of numbers showing that pages from your site rank on the first page of every major search engine. Most probably you'll see a couple of 1s, a 2 and maybe a No – and you can act immediately: why are you not ranked on Lycos or Netscape? Do you need to submit the site to them? What improvements can be made to your pages to ensure you're on page 1 across the board?

Run the test for every word or phrase that's important to your site, capture the data as a spreadsheet and run the test every month. Hopefully, as you continue to implement new ideas, you'll start to see a marked improvement.

Here's an idea for you

Don't look at your link popularity and say 'I need one hundred in-bound links, now'.
That's too overwhelming. Be realistic; try to add an in-bound link at a rate of one
or two a week – easier to manage and less depressing.

25

All links are not born equal

PageRank, relevance and are you trustworthy?

Steer clear of websites offering themselves to you. There's something not right there. Instead seek out potential partners, target them, woo them, strike...

Darwin and natural selection

PageRank is an important part of Google's ranking algorithm – some would say the most important aspect. The higher your PageRank, the higher your site will be ranked. The PageRank within your website is increased by pages from other sites linking to it, and the higher the PageRank of those pages the better it is for the recipient site – i.e. you. So in your hunt for in-bound links a handful of links from sites with a PageRanking of five or above is going to be of far more intrinsic value to you than hunting around for hundreds of low PageRanked sites. Be selective with your links – ten good ones are better than a hundred naff ones.

Yes, but what's the connection?

With in-bound links, obviously a high PageRank is important, but that's not the only contributory factor. There needs to be a relevance between the content on the website that's linking to you and your own site. It's not much good having a website with a PageRank of seven linking to you if you sell T-shirts and the referring site is a hotel directory. There's no connection, there's no relationship, basically there's no point...

Here's an idea for you

Believe it or not, there are websites out there who actively want links to your website. Type in one of your keywords or phrases and then type 'add URL'. For example when I was looking to promote my book *The Bloke's Guide To Pregnancy* I typed: 'pregnancy "add URL"'. I was then presented with numerous websites that had some connection to pregnancy and accepted URL submissions. Priceless.

This is a time consuming exercise. Some sites will want reciprocal links in exchange, some will want to charge you and some just don't work. Ignore all except those sites that allow you to add your URL with no strings attached – your perseverance will be rewarded. Within 72 hours the number of in-bound links will begin to rise, and if any of those linking sites have a high PageRank you could notice an increase to your own rank the next time the Googlebot pays a visit. You can repeat the exercise by searching for the keyword 'add link' and the keyword 'guestbook' to ensure you capture all of the sites out there offering you a chance to market your site.

No DMOZ, no champagne corks

The importance of the Open Directory Project

Solicit yourself to every directory, society, search engine, reference site and information portal that you can – if they're free, all the better. But DMOZ is the undisputed king...

www.dmoz.org

The Open Directory Project is a very unassuming website out there in cyberspace that carries a tremendous amount of weight. Its USP, ironically in this technical age, is that it is human powered and not software driven. DMOZ doesn't employ spiders to scan the web, it waits for you to submit your URL and then assigns an editor to check your listing manually and, assuming you've added yourself to the correct category, you'll be listed on DMOZ.

What's the point?

Very few users actually use the directory to conduct searches – why would you when Google does it so much better? – so being listed is not going to affect your traffic levels. DMOZ's data can be downloaded for free, and both small and large websites use that data to improve their own sites – and one of those sites is Google. In fact, Google's own directory is nothing other than the DMOZ data.

A successful listing on DMOZ creates two important links into a website – one from DMOZ and one from the Google Directory. Both DMOZ and Google have a very high PageRank. Add to this the thousands of links created by all the websites who are using the DMOZ directory and it becomes obvious why a listing in DMOZ is so important. It's often the case that a DMOZ listing alone will raise your PageRank by one or two!

Patience, dear boy

DMOZ's strength is also its weakness. As it is staffed by volunteers, there is a huge queue of websites clamouring to get listed and there are only so many hours in the day, so it can take up to eight weeks for your URL submission to be translated into a listing. Don't send snotty emails asking for an update or complaining about the delay, just sit tight and wait. If you've followed the instructions, your turn will come.

Here's an idea for you

You've guessed it, make it your job this afternoon to get on to DMOZ and submit your URL. Read the submission guidelines and choose your category wisely to avoid unnecessary delays.

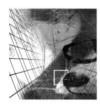
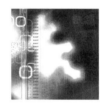

Google pretender?

Competition for the throne

There's loving Google and there's wanting to marry it. I love Google for the instant gratification it can give me today... but I certainly wouldn't want to marry it.

www.searchenginewatch.com

The one problem with search engine optimisation and particularly with Google is that it is a constantly changing phenomenon. As soon as too many people get wind of a certain facet – take, for example, the current importance of having a DMOZ.org listing – Google will eventually get the hump and alter its algorithm accordingly. For the web business owner it becomes a constant game of cat and mouse, forever searching out the latest techniques to help beat, no I mean *utilise*, the system.

The beauty of sites like ***www.searchenginewatch.com*** is that you will get the truth (or at least 'a' truth) about what's going on in the world of search engine marketing. Not content with Google's dominance, you can catch up on the latest findings regarding every major search engine and how it relates to your site. This online community, certainly at the time of writing, appears to have no political or software manufacturer allegiance – it's simply a meeting place of webmasters and website owners discussing their experiences and their concerns about search engine marketing and promotion. Two weeks of your life would be well spent exploring those posts and researching the archives.

Live search

I have various personal quibbles with Microsoft but, having said that, to not mention the behemoth and the emerging importance of Live search would detract from my message: keep your options open. Live search has gone through a number of facelifts recently but it basically represents a 2.0 version of MSN. Live search is fast, efficient and, as far as I am concerned, painfully accurate. Microsoft claims that its technology is unique and I believe it is; however, I find it difficult to find a website that ranks highly on Live search that doesn't also rank highly on Google – which suggests some similarities between the algorithms.

Here's an idea for you

It may seem like a waste of time, but it tends to follow that a site that fares well on Google tends to rank well on all the other search engines. Check! Do you really rank the same, if not better, on all the major search engines? Although Google should be your benchmark, don't neglect the competition.

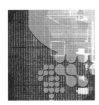 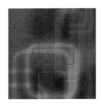 

28

Your website under the knife

You at the back, pay attention...

No one likes criticism, especially if someone else has been paid to do the work, but sometimes website errors creep in. Know what those errors are and start erasing them

Playing to the stalls

HTML and website design in general is a pretty organic process – new techniques grow and then become the norm; web browsers also grow in a bid to display this new code correctly. Conversely, old techniques become, well, old – no longer used and browsers no longer support them. If those techniques have been employed on your site, then as time goes on your website will become less and less accessible. So what can you do to stay abreast of what's hot and what's not?

Validate your HTML. You want your website to be accessible to the largest cross-section of Internet users as possible, and this means catering for all tastes and persuasions and not putting all your eggs into one basket. In an annoying way this also means catering for the lowest common denominator – the users who haven't updated their web browser, or their plug-ins, not because they've made a decision not to, but because they don't know how. Yet these users could be your biggest customers and the last thing you want to do is piss them off because they can't see your site...

W3C.org

The self-appointed guardians of HTML. W3C are an influential organisation and a friend of theirs is a friend of Google. I can't stress this enough: third-party accreditation and recognition is massively important to Google. If you follow W3C's validation instructions and pass, the validation logo you'll display on your site will be worth its weight in gold in terms of how the Googlebot regards your site from then on.

W3C are pretty anally retentive – for example I was pulled up on an error regarding one of my sites because it wasn't Internet Explorer version 4 compliant (Microsoft doesn't even support IE 4.X any more, so why on earth should I?). Take what they say seriously, but with a pinch of salt – sometimes it's form over function. If you can fix those errors, do so, and enjoy your new-found ally. It's been worth at least a PageRank jump of one place for many a website.

Here's an idea for you

Pay a visit to ***http://validator.w3.org***, type in the URL of your website and await the results. Hopefully, you'll pass in which case you'll be provided with a little bit of code that allows you to display the W3C validation logo on your site - I suppose it's the equivalent of an ISO 9001 for web design. A huge accolade, and one well worth shouting about. Of course, most of us won't pass on our first go and W3C kindly provide a comprehensive list of all the errors and, better yet, suggestions about how to fix them. Check out the following validation tools too: ***http://www.htmlvalidator.com*** and ***http://watson.addy.com***

29

Where next?

The site map and Google

**You must do everything in your power to help both waylaid
visitors and lost search engines when they find themselves
alone and without direction on your website.**

Do not pass go

Many webmasters argue that including a site map allows users to
bypass their well thought out navigation paths and that, therefore,
users aren't subjected to the full, all-powerful magic of the site.
Absolute rubbish. If your visitor cannot find, in a very limited
amount of time, what it is they want, then they are going to leave
– and probably not come back. If the Googlebot can't find a way
through your website then it's not going to hang around too long
either, and Google are certainly not going to contact you with a
follow-up courtesy call just to check everything's fine. You've had
your chance.

By offering a site map, yes, some users might miss out on great offers, witty copy and stunning images, but they do get to where they wanted to go. They might still partake in your promotions and appreciate your huge range, just not right now. Be patient. Likewise, if the Googlebot can index your entire site, which it can do easily through a site map, then it is going to help you rank higher on many more keyword searches. And that's what you want. Isn't it? Google can't follow your JavaScript navigation. Employing a site map ensures there's an obvious link to every page and the Googlebot will take the easy route if a site map is offered. If your site map is accurate Google will index every page presented.

Help! I need somebody

You can never reinforce things too many times on a website and it is therefore a shrewd manoeuvre to include the site map as part of your help page, even if it has its own link or button on the home page. Users do not think alike; some will spot the direct reference and others will assume that you have hidden it within the help pages. Most importantly, be sure that there is a direct link to the site map from the home or index page of your site.

Here's an idea for you

If you don't already have a site map, this must be addressed – no matter how small your site. Even if you have created your site using WYSIWYG (What You See Is What You Get) software, then a map can often be created automatically by the program and added as a page. If developers have created your site, you can ask them to map out the site, as this is information that they should already have created when they built the site in the first place. Lastly, you can get one free at **http://www.xml-sitemaps.com** (in return for advertising their service). If you already have a site map featured on your site, make sure that the locations are clickable and bring the user, and Google, to that page of your site.

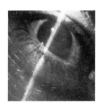
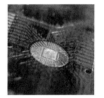

30

Rank and file

How are your keywords performing?

Pay attention there! It's no good hoping everything's just fine, so find out the truth about how well you please Google, you cheeky minx...

A leap above the competition – *www.marketleap.com*

This website probably proved invaluable when you were first researching your keywords and phrases earlier on. But the tool we need to focus on now is the keyword verification report. The process is simple; you enter your URL and the keyword or phrase you wish to be measured on, and the report returns whether you rank in the top three pages and on which of those pages you appear – i.e. ideally, you want to see page 1 on all six search engines. If your site ranks on page 4, or below, this is deemed as not ranking. Although not entirely accurate, the simple truth is that if you're not in the top three pages, it's unlikely anyone's going to drill down to your listing. Therefore you don't exist as far as those particular search engines are concerned. Worrying, isn't it?

Big boys' toys – *www.axandra.com*

Marketleap is a great tool (not least because it works, and it's free) but you and I are busy people. If you're only interested in monitoring a handful of keywords, then it serves its purpose with minimal investment from you. However, most of us are looking to monitor a large number of keywords and phrases and we would much rather technology took care of the donkey work: well, help is at hand. Pop over to ***www.axandra.com*** and download their Internet Business Promoter/Arelis software for a hardcore version of a keyword performance tool (and so much more). I can't sing their praises enough; IBP helps you with all-important aspects of on-site website promotion. It includes more than 15 professional website promotion tools, including tools for keyword generation, a top 10 search engine ranking optimisation, search engine submission, directory submission, ranking checking – and with the Arelis download you'll benefit from highly targeted free traffic to your website, new business contacts, a higher link popularity, higher search engine rankings and more sales... Yes, it's that good. In fact, if you could put it in a dress, I'd propose marriage!

Here's an idea for you

The good news is that you can download a limited demo version of IBP to test it out. The demo version allows you to automate your keyword performance, which is what you should do, immediately. So, you've tested your performance and you'll know one of two things very quickly - either your site is performing well with regard to your chosen keywords or it's not, and you will need to bring it up to speed. If you are ranked on page 1 for each of the major search engines, then by all means give yourself a pat on the back, but bear in mind that the Internet is a constantly changing phenomenon. Someone, somewhere, is gunning for your position...

31

Number crunching

Stats, stats and more stats

Number crunching is boring... you might think like this, but whether you like it or not your salvation and future wealth may lie within a humble spreadsheet...

We should take comfort from the fact that everything can be and is measured on the web. The trick is to pay attention to all of this information and to utilise it. Unlike any other market, the information is there for the taking: statistics about your site, your traffic, your users, where they come from, what they do on the site and where they go afterwards. All this is available if only we ask for it and, more importantly, want to understand it.

www.dataplain.com

Google Analytics is great but I also believe that variety is the spice of life. We have to assume that Google's intentions are morally just but we also have to bear in mind that it still remains a profit-hungry business that eats and despises its competition, and therefore we can't be 100% trusting of its product/s. For this reason if you haven't got a stats package as part of your website (as well as Analytics), I would strongly suggest investing in a third-party package to work alongside Analytics just to compare and contrast data. There are many packages on the market and a search for 'web statistics' will pull up many thousands of offerings. Dataplain is pretty slick and with the great British pound spanking the bottom of the US dollar at the moment, buy American – it's as cheap as fries.

Remember not everyone uses Google

I'm more conscious than most about rising up the rankings on Google and continually update my sites to stay ahead of the game. My sites rank well on all the search engines but the truth of the matter is that ***www.jonsmith.net*** gets most of its referred visitors from AltaVista, and ***www.justdads.co.uk*** gets more referred visitors from MSN/Live.com than Google.

This information is priceless because if my sites were commercial rather than information portals I would know to commit my resources to try and get noticed in terms of paid-for listings with Google. Conversely, Toytopia, the online toyshop my wife and I ran, received more than 90% of referred traffic from Google. That's why we spent most of our marketing budget advertising with Yahoo et al. – we didn't need to spend much with Google because we were doing so well there organically.

Here's an idea for you

Let's say you've decided to spend a modest £3 per day with Google AdWords. Give or take, that's an online marketing spend of £100 per month. Now, if we assume that Google have about 80% of the UK search market, then all the others make up a considerable 20%. Match your spend to this trend. Allocate £0.60 per day across the other engines (your stats will tell you who to invest with) and see what happens. Four to eight weeks of activity will ascertain whether it's worth investing more or less – and for the grand sum of about £30.

32

IP city

Location management in a virtual world

Despite the global reach of the Internet, sometimes it's best to call home... your home.

Where you call home...

As a UK-based business, the two sexiest domain names you can own are .co.uk and .com. For whatever reason they might be both gone and you're left with the dregs. If .net has gone give up the search and start again. Investing your money in .gb.eu.com is a complete waste of time – ones like this look clunky, users find them difficult to remember and there is a suspicion that the business is a bit fly by night. Yes, there are a handful of businesses that have made .biz or .tv a success, but for every one of those, there are at least 500 successful .co.uk or .com sites.

Home and away

It's very easy to buy domain names from the comfort of your own home. That's the easy bit. The difficult bit is ensuring that they are registered/hosted in the appropriate country. If you are trying to appeal to a UK audience be sure that your hosting partner's servers are based in the UK, and that they're not just a reseller for an American hosting firm. Likewise, if you're after the Irish market, host your website in Ireland. Google knows where the servers are and will automatically favour your website in that country's search results – which may not be your target market.

IP and your user

When a user visits your site, unless they buy something, register with the site or contact you for information, you've no real idea who they are. The only thing they leave behind is their IP address – a numerical code that in crude terms represents the user's computer. This doesn't tell you a lot, but it does reveal their location, and this is important. Now, it might not have been your intention but if the majority of your users are from the US or France or Australia you would do well to relaunch a localised site in that country. If these customers are finding you and using you despite the hidden barriers, imagine the potential of a site that's optimised for them. Want to know which country your visitors are coming from? Check out ***http://www.ip2location.com/free.asp***

Here's an idea for you

Work through your WHOIS details and ascertain exactly where your domain names were registered and, more importantly, where they are currently hosted. You probably went for the cheapest and easiest option at the time – I did too – but that doesn't mean it was the best option.

33

Treating users and Google differently

E-commerce and the session ID curse...

A dynamic website is the fastest way to offer good, relevant and exciting content to your customers, but Google finds a dynamic site hard to index – what should you do?

Who's your audience?

You should create your website for your user first and Google second. Sometimes these two separate audiences relate and react positively to the same thing, but your focus should always be on the human user with Google a close second – and not the other way round. At the end of the day whilst Google might give you the exposure, it's never going to buy anything from you, ever. Talk to your potential client on every occasion, whilst keeping the search engine happy.

Bring the noise

The problem most e-commerce websites have with Google is the sheer vast amount of catalogue or products carried. We faced the same problem with our toy store – with a modest 150 products, by the time we'd included size options, colour preferences, personalisation, gift messages, various forms of shipping and what wrapping the customer would like we had an enormous database of product, or at least it was enormous as far as the search engines were concerned. On top of that, we wanted to recognise users as they visited the site so that we could capitalise on their next visit – that's why we employed the session ID. That's probably why you've employed it too.

The only problem is that Google doesn't really like the session ID because as far as it's concerned it means a new page that needs to be indexed, even though it has been there before. In fact, the very nature of session IDs is that the same product or page Google has been to before could have infinite session IDs – and that's why it doesn't like them one bit.

Why the rage?

As far as Google is concerned, or any other search engine, for that matter, the session ID offers content (which may have already been indexed) at a new location. Every time the Googlebot visits, that same content could appear under a different guise/session ID and therefore, rather than wasting resources and maybe double-indexing the same information, Google chooses to ignore it. The Googlebot would rather just bypass the whole potential mess and turn its back on a page when it spots an '&' in the address.

Here's an idea for you

Altering the fundamental structure of your website is a massive request – but having said that, I would still recommend it. If it's any consolation Google acknowledges what a pain in the arse it might prove to be and for the first and only time admits to encouraging what constitutes a 'cloaked' page – i.e. a page that Google sees as being different to one the general public sees. That means that you can serve a page to the general public including a session ID (so that you can maximise the marketing potential of that customer) whilst at the same time offer the same page to the Googlebot without the session ID, and get away with it. Bizarre, I know.

34

Web design #404

'Page cannot be found' suicide

Click, click, click, ohhh? If I click on a link I expect it to work. A 'page cannot be found' error results in your user abandoning your site, never to return...

Netmechanic

This is such a great tool, and if you're happy to check one web page at a time, absolutely free! Netmechanic tests the technical functions of your site and within a few seconds you will receive some important feedback about how well your site performs, so check out *www.netmechanic.com/products/HTML_Toolbox_Free Sample.shtml*

Load time

How fast is the server serving up the pages? How many servers need to be contacted for the user to download files and images? Are your images optimised for the web? Whilst the vast majority of users are employing broadband, they'll only be so forgiving when waiting for a new site to load. Note that Netmechanic penalises sites with web pages over 40k in size, which is a bit draconian. Most importantly, Google is only going to serve up search results which will allow their customers to get to information quickly.

HTML check and repair

This is not as in-depth as the W3C.org facility, but is a great starting point in terms of whether the code behind your site is fit for purpose. If there are errors, Netmechanic will even suggest how to fix them. Google will penalise sites with clunky or error-ridden code. Why on earth would Google want to serve up bad pages to its own customers?

Browser compatibility

Not everyone uses Internet Explorer (or PCs for that matter) and the number of people choosing to turn their backs on Microsoft products is growing at an astounding rate every month. You and your web developer need to be aware of how your site looks across all the major browsers, because the difference can be enormous. Browsers such as Netscape, Opera and Firefox are all free downloads and if you're not a convert already I would strongly suggest you move over to Firefox at your earliest convenience. If you haven't got access to a Mac, be sure to have a friend or colleague check out your site using the Safari browser. If your site looks weird, users aren't going to hang around.

Link check

OK, so Netmechanic can't tell if all the links are going to the right page, but what it's looking for are Error #404s – page cannot be found. Broken or dead links are messy, an annoyance for users and if you serve one of them up expect to lose that user instantaneously. No one is going to take time out of a busy schedule to send you a polite little email highlighting the fault. It's up to you to stay on top of this, and now you have the tool to do it.

Here's an idea for you

You've tested your own site using Netmechanic, now why not use it to spy on your competition? How do they fare in comparison? Is it possible to see a relationship between their current Google positioning and the faults found by Netmechanic? This sort of competitive analysis is priceless, yet available for free with a few clicks of the mouse!

35

How clean is your house?

Non-smoking, professional, clean code only

Dig out the Marigolds (don't attempt anything without the gloves) and get down and dirty, Kim and Aggie style, with the code behind your site.

Tidy house, tidy mind

Google is a fussy guest; it doesn't want to see flock wallpaper and retro light fittings – it wants to see clean lines, minimal clutter and impeccably bright surfaces. So, how does this translate in terms of code? Well, for starters, check out what Google says at http://www.google.co.uk/support/webmasters/#label which gives clear and uncompromising instructions on what Google's expecting from your site.

In a nutshell, Google prefers you to present your code in a logical manner – and that logic is clear delineation between the showy presentation components of the page and the core content.

Google's early visits to your site will be glancing at best and if your code is presented logically, Google will be inclined to return; if your code meanders, the Googlebot will get bored sifting through the flotsam and jetsam and move on. Less is more.

A topsy-turvy site

Now this might upset your developer, but it is worth broaching the subject with them about the layout of the code that makes up your site – if at all possible what you are looking for is almost a reversal of how things are normally done. For example, the classic and, I suppose, the logical way to build a web page has the same principles as building a house – you start with the foundations, build the walls, put on a roof and at the last stage deal with putting in some furniture. But bearing in mind the importance Google places on content (read furniture) you might want to give this more importance earlier on in the build. In an ideal world, therefore, after the header information, you want to be straight into content (including keywords, H tags, Alt tags etc) and then the architecture – or the showy presentation bit – follows afterwards.

Labels, labels, labels

Labelling is everything as far as Google is concerned. The Googlebot is looking for flags that accurately represent and showcase the body copy you've used on the page. Tell Google how you've organised the page and what importance you place on certain sections – H, or header, tags work if you prioritise them correctly along with good use of Alt tags on your images. Rather than splitting text with a simple break (<BR>) command, use a paragraph marker (<P>), and highlight to Google where it should be looking and what the focus should be.

Here's an idea for you

Pay a visit to the source code behind your site (exactly how you do this will depend on your browser and whether you're using a PC or a Mac). You will be generally presented with a pop-up notepad page showing the code behind that page. Whether or not the content means anything to you, does it look neat and orderly or is it one continuous line of code all jumbled together? If it's the latter, have the developer neaten it up.

36

JavaScript intolerance

Cookies and a lack of appetite

You can get all gourmet with Google, offer up hand-picked scallops and fresh basil, but what it wants for its sustenance is a simple slice of toast...

Not a chocolate chip in sight – call that a cookie?

An HTML cookie is nothing more than a packet of text sent by the server (along with the page being served up) that is immediately sent back to the server. What it does is allow the site to remember a customer's behaviour, patterns and actions. For instance, if you previously placed a book entitled *Web Sites That Work* into your shopping basket, then the next time you return the site recognises you and that item remains in your basket. Without cookies you'd be regarded as a brand new customer.

At this level cookies are fine, but what if you've employed cookies to ascertain that someone has signed in, or has paid a subscription to access certain parts of your website? Well, Google can't and won't process cookies and therefore cannot access these 'members only' pages. What's worse is that Google won't give you the benefit of the doubt – it will assume that you are employing cloaking techniques (i.e. one page served up to human users and another served up to Google). As far as Google is concerned this is inherently wrong, and the reaction is to penalise the site. Avoid cookies where you can.

JavaScript

It makes navigation sexy, but ironically it currently cloaks the content from Google's all-seeing burning eye... Basically Google recognises how sexy JavaScript can be but also recognises, in its benevolent heart, that it might not be accessible to every visitor (those too lazy or ignorant to download JavaScript runtime). Therefore Google will always penalise JavaScript-heavy sites – unless you have the foresight to incorporate a pure HTML or XML site map, accessible from the home page, that will allow Google to index the entire site regardless of the implementation of JavaScript.

Oh, the irony

In a strange twist of fate it has become apparent that users who do not have JavaScript enabled on their web browsers may find it difficult to fully access Google's AdWords in terms of how the adverts are actually displayed. Why, oh why is Google so blind to the fact that most web users are going to want JavaScript-enabled sites? Surely they could incorporate a reader into the Googlebot to acknowledge this, and therefore display sites that do employ elements of JavaScript with the same gusto as sites that are constructed out of pure HTML...

Here's an idea for you

So you look at your source code and very quickly realise that all of that funky navigation and all those roll-over graphics are wholly dependent on JavaScript. It's going to hurt, it's probably going to cost too, but get rid of them. A difficult bullet to bite, but when it comes to the question of to whom you should be tailoring your site, human users can see JavaScript and text-based links. Google can only see text-based links. It doesn't take a genius to work out what has universal appeal...

37

The bigger picture

Cash poor, time poor? click here...

So, you haven't got the extra capital to employ an SEO specialist to monitor everything for you? Don't worry; help is at hand.

www.statcounter.com

Yes, it's another stats package giving you the ability to see what's going on throughout your website. Are the keywords and phrases that you've invested so much time (and possibly money) into actually working? Yes, Google Analytics gives you information, but it's only truly accurate for activity on a Google search. Everything else is banded into Yahoo!, or AltaVista, but if you're investing time and money with these other search engines, you're going to want to know how everything is performing in one glance – and that's what Statcounter provides.

123

Which search engines are performing for us?

Google, I've stressed before, is the market leader at the moment, and may well be forever more – but may not be. Don't ignore the old hands and certainly don't ignore the new smaller players as they appear on the market; Google was a small player not so long ago. Keep a close eye on the non-Google stats. Is there a pattern forming and is traffic increasing, even by just 1% a month? They may not be world-beating search engines, but they might be working very well for your site and your business.

Elvis has left the building

What I really like about Statcounter that you don't get with Google Analytics is the exit page analysis. This simply tracks the last page a visitor was reading before they decided to abandon your website for new climes. Now, if you run an information-based website rather than an e-commerce site, then one would hope that the highest ranking exit page would be your contact us page – indicating that the user has gleaned the information required, then found your contact details and either emailed you or picked up the phone. Is this the case?

Here's an idea for you

Something that will work with either Statcounter or Google Analytics is reacting to the visitor location information. It may be that you thought that your product would do well in Ireland; you're in the UK, there's only a little distance involved and the products you sell should do really well over there. The truth of the matter is, according to your stats, that this is not the case; there seems to a strong interest in your products from Belgium (of all places!) where customers are already finding you and ordering product. Imagine how much stronger that offering could be with a bit of page optimisation and even a bit of an AdWords spend? Sometimes stats throw your business plan on its head. Whilst that's a shock to the system – it's always quite hard to swallow the fact that you might be wrong – let the sales figures be the judge and, your pride aside, react accordingly.

38

Deep, deep down

Understanding the long tail

How big is your market? What do people want? Do you even know? When did you last sit down with your customer hat on? What does Google think of that?

The easy way, and the long way

When we all start out planning our own business we want to sell what's popular, be that a service or a product. The public like *Teletubbies*, so that's what we'll sell. But there's no money in it – out there is a competitor who can either buy the product cheaper, or sell it cheaper, and still make money. So where does that leave you? High and dry is the simple answer. Think outside of the box: would that customer also be interested in other educational programme merchandise? What about board games, or posters, or rival characters and properties? The long tail is all about taking a theme and working

126

it through to the very end. A customer interested in Harry Potter books might also be interested in a science kit... at first glance it's a tenuous link, but you're not going to compete with Amazon et al. selling the book or the DVD, so why not profit from the ancillary products – the magic kit, the magic wand, the magic cape?

Simple economics

You can spend your life promoting and selling the popular items on your site, but market forces will dictate that you have to sell these at a bigger discount than your competitors – and sell a whole lot more of them to make a profit because they're so cheap elsewhere. Seek the long tail in terms of what it is that you should actually sell. I think your buying skills are intrinsically related to what your attitude should be in terms of how you promote the website. Unless you have multimillion-pound backing there's no point going for the generic market, no matter what your field of expertise.

Turn to the niche market. It might be small (by definition) but with it comes passion, brand loyalty and often an obsession unequivocal in any other sense. Look at the obsession with sci-fi character figurines – as a hard-core fan would you wake up one day and buy from a conglomerate such as Toys'R'Us, or would you buy through a small website with a community aspect to it that you've been involved in for the last few months? Even if that same product costs you a few pounds more?

Here's an idea for you

Return to your keyword analysis. Were there products, phrases or sentiments that indicated you could expand or alter your offering? Don't ignore what the facts are, even if it goes against the very reasons you decided to set up your company. Profit first, integrity second.

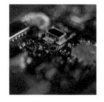

39

Feeding hungry eyes

Forums, communities and RSS

A sticky site is one in which users feel happy spending time and feel they have a reason to return to again and again.

If you can create a community feeling on your site, you will reap the rewards in terms of numbers of visitors and consumers, whatever you are selling or promoting on the web. Google will notice this activity and will also note the many mentions of keywords related to your market being mentioned on a daily basis. Every time the Googlebot visits there's tonnes of relevant, new and original content – guess what's going to happen to your ranking?

A home from home

When it comes to comfort we would all much prefer a soft and luxurious hotel duvet than a starchy, stained motel blanket. This is the feeling you need to replicate for users. Envelop them in your expertise and knowledge, convince the world that your website is the definitive provider of information or products and give them a nice warm feeling – all that makes it nigh on impossible to leave. When users feel relaxed and at ease they will automatically want to spend more time on your site, and if there is something to buy, then hands are going to be reaching into wallets. And never underestimate the power of word of mouth. With the propensity of chat rooms, discussion boards, forums and blogs, it does not take long for news to get around. Hopefully, users will be so impressed with your site and your service that they will be telling all their friends.

We're not really in the right market for forums

Cars are easy, they're popular, but what about my dental website, or my engineering firm? Well, we're back to a phrase that was popular in the late 90s – 'content is king' – and it really is. If your site has great copy, which is updated regularly and is of interest to users, then they're going to want to read it. If there's a forum that appears to be well used they'll be inclined to join in: 'I didn't know there were so many people interested in collecting beer mats'. With the invention of RSS feeds, the hard work is done for you. You post a message or an article and those who've signed up get a feed – and if there are links on the feed they come back to visit your site.

Here's an idea for you

Look on the web and find some open source forums that can be downloaded. For starters you can check out http://www.phpbb.com. Compare the specifications, especially the ability to customise, the appearance (if any) of third-party advertisers and any issues regarding users having to download a plug-in to take part on the message board. Assuming you have found some suitable software, look to adding it on to the site – at first, this could be left hidden from public view, until you have configured it, tested the functionality and filled it with legitimate messages from your huge customer base. Don't think forums are only suitable for B2C (business to consumer) websites. They can be incredibly effective additions to B2B (business to business) sites, too, by allowing clients to post messages to other clients.

40

Switching on targeting computer...

Good and bad navigation

The Force may well have worked for Luke Skywalker, but your users are not Jedi... they need to be shown a clear, well-defined path that they can follow.

Navigate this, if you can

Keyword prominence and relevance should be your primary concern in terms of creating effective copy for a website, but it all starts with the navigation on the site. You have to be clear and concise in your offering. JavaScript has its place but Google can't see it, which means that in lieu of a site map it can't index your site; the Googlebot will just get stuck on your home page. Graphical representations of buttons look great, but Google can't see the words you added to the graphics making those links redundant. Simple, honest text links work well for human users and robots. Anything else is actually detrimental to your site and its potential to be ranked.

Irrelevant navigation

Most website design aficionados will sing the praises of keeping your navigation consistent throughout a site to promote familiarity and ease of use, but Google doesn't need its hand held so tightly – in fact, it would prefer it if the navigational options altered as it entered different sections or areas of the site. For example, let's say you have a B2C and a B2B offering on your website. You will always rank higher on Google if the navigation alters depending on the section of the site users find themselves in. Your navigation should always be subject specific and dense in relevant and related keywords. If I'm in the personal banking section of a website, there's no need to show me your business banking options – they're irrelevant to me and to Google.

The three click rule

It dates back to the dawn of the Internet, but remains true even today – your user needs to conclude a visit to your site within three clicks of the mouse. If you're selling products then that third click should be adding the item to their basket. If your site is primarily there to provide information and prospecting for new clients, then that third click should be to your contact us page or to an online enquiry form. If it currently takes longer than three clicks for a user to complete their interaction with your site, then you must revisit the process.

Here's an idea for you

Pop over to Amazon and place an order for *Web Sites That Work* or any other book that takes your fancy. As you go through the order pipeline (the pages between adding the item to your basket and paying for it) you'll see a very simple graphic at the top of the page that represents the stages involved and where you currently are. Ingenious. A simple device that both reassures users that this process won't take long and a visual hint to where they currently are in the proceedings. Add something similar to your site immediately.

41

The WORLD wide web

Running a multilingual website marketing campaign

The entire world does not speak English. By ignoring other languages, you are in effect blocking potential users from finding and interacting with your business.

Speaking in tongues

We are very lucky that English is often regarded as the language of both the net and business, but we have to remind ourselves that not everyone speaks it. Non-English versions of a website are not created overnight, nor will the cost of translation be cheap. Taking the step to offer a multilingual site, or dedicated language versions, is something that has to involve all functions of the business and must be budgeted for. The overriding question must be whether a multilingual version of your website, or launching a new country-specific site, will add value for both yourself and your customers. If the answer is no, save yourself the project management nightmare and spend the money visiting these far-off climes instead.

Going the whole hog

If you decide you need, or have already implemented, a multilingual site, well done! Multilingual sites are difficult projects to manage and maintain, but the benefits – if they are done correctly – can be immense. Be sure to assign a country manager to each language version of the site/s. This person will be responsible for the website content and updates but, more importantly, will be your interface with the local Google site. They will have to manage keyword selection, optimisation, and an AdWords budget if you are planning to pay for placement.

Managing multilingual campaigns

Follow the same steps as you would for your English-language site. Find out who your competitors are, research your keywords and begin optimising the non-English pages. You will need to set up an account with each of the Google territories to monitor your AdWord and Analytics; for Spain, for instance, you would start with www.google.es.

Here's an idea for you

Make a business case for your site to be translated into two additional languages. What would be the benefits to the company, which two languages would be best and what competition are you facing from websites written in those languages and operating in those countries? The plan may well show that making your site multilingual is not a viable option. However, it could reveal a huge opportunity (like there not being a single company selling the same products you sell in the whole of Spain) that could easily be exploited.

42

No rest for the wicked

Refining, retuning, rediscovering...

Once most of the hard work is done a common mistake is to sit back, hoping the good times just keep happening. They won't, unless you stay on top of the game.

Newbie alert

New players are coming on to the scene every minute. You're not the only company selling garden gnomes on the web, and if you are today, you won't be tomorrow. Don't rest on your laurels; your great page ranking is only good for that one day – who knows what's going to occur tomorrow or next week?

Why the fluctuation?

OK, so you've finally begun to reap the rewards – a presence on page 1 of the keywords that are important to you and the increase in traffic and business that you have been after, for so long. Then one day you're not there, knocked off your perch and banished to the depths of page 2, or worse. How? Why? Well, don't forget that many of your rivals and any new players in the market who are aware of the importance of SEO will be tweaking their sites too, but most importantly the search engines themselves are forever altering their algorithms. Therefore, what was sexy yesterday (think reciprocal links) has been replaced by something else today (think in-bound links). Just be aware that the web and search engines are a constantly changing phenomenon and that it's your responsibility to keep abreast of what's hot and what's not. The web and the rules that govern it are organic – and it's that very fact that keeps it exciting and incredibly modern but, conversely, incredibly frustrating for website owners.

Here's an idea for you

Every six months (more frequently if you own a large, content-rich site) you should be looking to evaluate and consider your website and its performance. Treat the site as you would an employee (regular beatings, denial of holidays and Morning Coffee biscuits in the canteen instead of Chocolate Hob Nobs). Involve your staff in this process and have them test the site thoroughly. Within a matter of hours you should have a comprehensive 'State Of The Nation' report that can be acted upon.

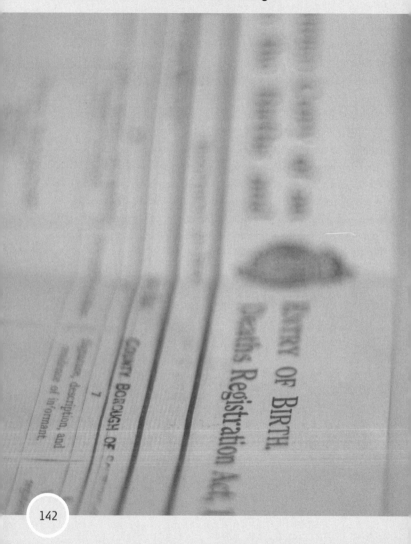

43

Naming the child

Web addresses and the importance of first names

Google is very unassuming in what it wants – to be dealing with one website on a first name terms basis. Anything that deviates from this mould gets it all flustered.

Registering births, deaths and marriages

There is a temptation, on larger sites, to rationalise the pages by creating sub-domains to better organise the content – for example using something like www.business.mydomain.com and www.personal.mydomain.com – but this is counter-productive. Google is much more of a fan of first names than last names and would prefer to see something like www.mydomain.com/business instead, which effectively does the same job for you and your users but keeps a smile on the face of Google. As your business expands and new categories or products make an appearance you just need to add another page – www.mydomain.com/newpage – and you can have as many as you like, it doesn't matter.

SKU = skewed

For ease of management I'm guessing that all of your products and services have been assigned stock keeping units (SKUs) or product IDs or some form of coding that means you know what it is, but everyone else doesn't, including Google. SKUs are obviously important to any retail business in terms of rationalising stock, orders, fulfilment and accounting – but Google and your users have no idea what an F22451 actually is. We'd all much prefer to know that it's a Sony 32-inch HD-ready LCD television, and that needs to be represented in the domain name of the page carrying that item.

Yes, but what do you mean?

So someone has searched for 'Sony 32-inch HD' on Google and is awaiting the results. Less than half a second later they are presented with a list. If you've named your product with a SKU then the chances of www.mydomain.com/F22451 being returned on page 1 are pretty slim. However, if you've named your page www.mydomain.com/Sony_32inch_HD-ready_LCD then it's got a far better chance of being shown to that potential user: a potential sale.

Here's an idea for you

Where it's possible, rename the web pages that carry your major products/services on your site to include the keywords that users will actually use to find that product. SKUs should be an internal referencing tool, not public information. Keep SKUs private, something management can throw into meetings to appear all knowledgeable – 'I see sales of 2234 have increased by 20% this month' – when the rest of the world would say 'we're selling a lot more bananas this month'.

44

Knowing Google

Dinner party secrets you can reveal...

Google, every now and again, releases information to assist web owners in improving their listings. These titbits are few and far between, so devour them when you can... better yet, drop them into conversation with other website owners for lashings and lashings of kudos.

How do I know if Google's been in town?

Depending on your stat package, you'll either see a reference on your stats to the Googlebot, or more likely, you'll see a huge list of IP addresses that don't seem to make an awful lot of sense. Worry not! Help is at hand. Here are the IP addresses you should be looking out for – if you see one of these, the Googlebot's paid you a visit:

64.68.80.#
64.68.81.#
64.68.82.#

64.68.84.#
64.68.88.#
216.239.46.#
216.239.38.#
216.239.36.#

unavailable_after

At the time of writing, the word on the Google grapevine was buzzing around the introduction of a new metatag for web-business owners to employ when they may want to flag the fact that they have time sensitive pages – for example Christmas offers, month-specific content or promotional information about an event. The basic idea is that if you have a page on your website that has an expiry date, you don't really want that page to be indexed after that date, and therefore being returned to Google searchers months after the content is no longer relevant. After all there's no point teasing customers with a potential 20% saving on all purchases in December if it's now June and the promotion has ended!

Some web owners would argue it's still better for an out of date page to be indexed and available to potential customers than not, but I don't think that pulling customers in on the promise of a discount that is no longer available, or an event that has been and gone is going to win you any friends at all.

Here's an idea for you

So you've read everything I've written; are you now armed and dangerous? Sort of, but as you've noticed yourself over the past few years, the web is a constantly changing phenomenon. Just look above to see the release of a new metatag that was previously unheard of. This will keep happening. The solution? Get involved and sign up to search engine blogs and emails to stay ahead of the game. The information is out there – that's the beauty of the web. Stay on top, stay informed – watch, look, listen: ***http:/www.searchenginejournal.com***

45

It's my party

Inviting links, without seeming desperate

It's going to require your best poker face – asking for links to your site whilst giving nothing in return…You could win, in the long run.

Phat spoilers

So, I meet with a client who runs a website that sells specialist body kits for boy-racer cars – Renault 5s, Subarus, Zafiras, etc. and things are going well, but could be better. We enter into a discussion about in-bound links and their importance and I suggest that the business owner should start getting involved in forums relating to his industry. 'But I'm already a member of loads,' he replies.

And he wasn't joking. Over the last three or so years he'd posted somewhere in the region of 5000 posts across a whole load of forums and chat rooms. Now, the beauty of forums is that more often than not they allow the user to create a profile, and one of the fields is URL. Most people leave this blank or add a link to their

FaceBook/MySpace page – such a waste. Add your company website address. In the case of the company above, he sold kit parts for cars and here he was chatting on performance-car-related sites. He quickly added the URL of the business to his profile and, being dynamic, the forums updated every post this chap had ever placed on their sites with a link to his own website. With over 5000 in-bound relevant links to his credit, his site became an authority site overnight with a PageRank of 7. From page 8 to page 1 in 24 hours. It brings a tear to my eye.

Beware: cash for honours

It damaged the major UK political parties and it could affect you too – there is an increasing trend for websites with a high PageRank to prostitute themselves to the highest bidder. Never mind selling a £10 DVD when you can sell your Google reputation for pounds and pounds and pounds. Google is wise to this tactic, and whilst I don't fully understand how it could possibly know that you and I exchanged a brown envelope in a service station café on the M1, it does. Buying in-bound links is a short-term fix and you'll be found out, which inevitably leads to all the punitive measures Google has at its disposal. Get to your goal through your own strengths and Google will reward you.

Here's an idea for you

If it hasn't dawned on you already, get searching on the web for a forum that's related to your industry. There's something out there for every taste and persuasion and if there really isn't, then there's your cue to add a forum or blog to your own site. I'm serious. Even if you run a website that focuses on welding, there's a potential market out there who would be keen to get involved; they're just waiting for a suitable venue. Become the authority site.

46

Yahoo! and industry-specific directories

Promiscuity rewarded

Put yourself about, don't be shy, don't shun the pimps. Know yourself for what you are – an e-prostitute...

Entertaining the masses

The other search engines are not to be sniffed at – it's all very well being number 1 on Google but, truth be told, although 80% of the search market is Google-led, that still leaves a massive 1 in 5 of Internet searchers who choose not to use Google, for whatever reason. Are you just as high on Live.com, Yahoo! or AskJeeves? If not, work on why not. Theoretically, if you rank highly on Google!, you also rank highly on the others – but this isn't always the case. In the past, if I'm honest, I've had sites that have ranked highly on every site *but* Google.

Business directories

They're out there and they are used – they just don't advertise themselves very well. Every city or county council will have a register or list of companies/businesses in the area and most offer a chance for you to add yourself or at least alter the information held on your business. I still receive queries via Bedford City Council's site from people interested in Toytopia Ltd; the business was sold four years ago and ceased trading soon afterwards, and yet they still come. These sites do work, so be sure you and your business are listed.

Twice-weekly bin collections... and your website

So we all hate our local councils – unruly youths allowed to roam the streets knocking off wing-mirrors and throwing empty bottles of cider into your garden... they're crap! But that said, completely different departments look after social issues to those which are interested in promoting local businesses, local interest and local innovation.

Use and talk to your local council about what it is you are doing as they're always keen to sing the praises of businesses within their region. At worst they'll add you to their directory which is another in-bound link; at best they will shower you with business advice, assistance (possibly financial) and will try to sing your praises (to make themselves look better) to the local press – which can only mean good exposure.

Here's an idea for you

Run a report through www.marketleap.com and take a look at which search engines have and haven't picked you up. I can't stress this enough: although Google is the daddy at the moment, this could all change very rapidly (probably through copyright holders suing for billions of dollars now that Google owns YouTube). Pay as much attention to your listing on AltaVista, AskJeeves et al. and you'll be ready for whatever revolution is about to happen. Make sure you're listed on every search engine and directory.

47
Negative press
Being dissed on the web

No matter how well you promote your business and your site, someone, somewhere might have it in for you... a disgruntled customer, an ex-employee, an obnoxious member of the public...

Disgruntled customers, whether they've explained their problem to you or not, may decide to use the web to vent their spleen; sometimes they'll write negative comments about a company in their blogs. Some of your competitors might like to damage your reputation by creating fake comments about your site.

No matter how good your company is, some people will always write something negative about your site, even if you tried your best to help them. What can you do if web pages with negative comments appear on the first result page for your company name?

Ask, and thou shalt receive...

That's not as unlikely as it might first appear. All webmasters are conscious about rankings and SEO and are striving to be the highest in their own field. If you were to send the webmaster of the web page in question a polite email and ask for the removal of the negative comments, they might very well agree – especially if this is a portal or forum site in which they have no control over the quality or accuracy of the comments submitted. Be friendly, polite, self-effacing and don't ever threaten the other person. Many webmasters will cooperate if you explain the issue.

Give web pages with positive comments about you a boost

Find websites that contain postive comments about your site, be they links, comments or testimonials. Link to these pages from your own site to increase the link popularity of these particular pages. The web pages with the positive comments might get more in-bound links and higher rankings, thus forcing them to leapfrog over the site with the negative comments. Granted, this is counter-productive to establishing your site as the number 1 site, but if you're a long way off, better the devil you know...

Wikipedia

Websites like ***www.AboutUs.org*** allow you to create an article about your own company. If your company is regarded as important enough, you might even find a page is created as an entry in Wikipedia. These 'Wiki' pages will be returned when someone searches for your company name. Having a reference on Wikipedia is tantamount to being featured as a guest voice on *The Simpsons* – it means you've made it, culturally. You're now a talking point and will soon enjoy your own listing in the *Oxford English Dictionary*. None of this is guaranteed, of course, but you never know...

Here's an idea for you

OK, so it's frowned upon, but who else is going to create a page about you on Wikipedia other than yourself? Fine, that's settled. It's pretty clear that you're the one that's going to have to do it. Learn the ropes, read the FAQs and get creating. Be sure to register with a name and email unrelated to your company and be sure to back up every fact and statement with a legitimate web link, source or external reference that can be verified.

48

What? Explain!

SEO in a nutshell

This is all very well, but if you could summarise what it is I have to do to make my site rock...

The German company Sistrix took it upon themselves to analyse web page elements of the top-ranked pages in Google to find out which specific elements lead to high Google rankings. They analysed 10,000 random keywords, and for every keyword, they analysed the top 100 Google search results.[1]

Which web page elements lead to high Google rankings?
Sistrix analysed the influence of the following elements: web page title, web page body, headline tags, bold and strong tags, image file names, images alt text, domain name, path, parameters, file size, in-bound links and PageRank.

1. Source: ***www.Axandra.com***

Keywords in the title tag seem to be important for high rankings on Google. It is also important that the targeted keywords are mentioned in the body tag, although the title tag seems to be more important.

Keywords in H2–H6 headline tags seem to have an influence on the rankings while keywords in H1 headline tags don't seem to have an effect.

Using keywords in bold or strong tags seems to have a slight effect on the top rankings. Web pages that used the keywords in image file names often had higher rankings. The same seems to be true for keywords in image alt attributes.

Websites that use the targeted keyword in the domain name often had high rankings. It might be that these sites get many in-bound links with the domain name as the link text.

Keywords in the file path don't seem to have a positive effect on the Google rankings of the analysed web sites. Web pages that use very few parameters in the URL (?id=123, etc.) or no parameters at all tend to get higher rankings than those URLs that contain many parameters.

The file size doesn't seem to influence the ranking of a web page on Google, although smaller sites tend to have slightly higher rankings.

It's no surprise that the number of in-bound links and the PageRank had a large influence on the page rankings on Google. The top result on Google has usually about four times as many links as result number 11.

Here's an idea for you

Look at, or have your developer look at, the use of (or lack of), header keywords within the code behind the site. If you have a number of H1 tags, look to split these up, in order of importance, into H1–H6 tags. If there are no header tags at all, then create some immediately but don't attribute all of them to the H1 status; sometimes less is more.

49

Google AdWords

Pay to be first

I've followed the advice and now I'm visible on page 1, I might even be the number 1 site for certain keywords, but what can I do next?

Why AdWords?

Google, you must remember, is a business. It does not provide this powerful search tool and employ thousands of staff around the world for a bit of fun. There are shareholders to appease, and that means Google needs to make money. Unlike other search engines, Google had a different approach from the start; its home page has always been dedicated to Google tools, not big-spend advertisers. This clean, uncluttered approach immediately made it attractive to users intent on searching. So where does it make money?

What Google has done with AdWords is essentially create an online auction of every word and phrase in every language – pretty incredible. No one's obliged to take part, but human nature is competitive (and lazy) and therefore when we see a competitor sitting proud at the very top or on the right of a search results page, we want to be there too. The more popular a keyword, the more the price goes up – and this is how Google makes its money: hundreds of thousands, if not millions, of businesses around the world (big and small) all paying their pennies and pounds for a little cameo in the top tier.

www.google.com/adwords

Set up is really simple, but do take the time to read the help and FAQs provided on the site. Google knows how its system works and has taken the time to explain it all; it just requires you to sit down, uninterrupted, to read through the data and see how it applies to your website and your industry. AdWords does work, but depending on your industry the current price for some keywords (such as Business Consultant or Microsoft Software Training) can be so high that it's prohibitive.

AdWords works by charging you a fee that you've decided upon every time someone clicks on your advert. The more you are willing to pay, the higher up the sponsored links you will be placed and the bigger your daily budget, the more users will be shown your advert and the more who will (hopefully) click through. As soon as your budget has been spent, your advert is taken off until the next day. This allows businesses to keep tight control of their online marketing spend and also allows you to see very quickly if the campaign is working and judge your return on investment.

Here's an idea for you

Google AdWords really is instantaneous – you sign up, create an advert, give them your credit card details and that's it. Your advert will be displayed immediately to users searching for that particular keyword in the territories you've selected. Set yourself a really low budget, say £1.00 per day, and your advert will be shown until that budget has been spent. Again, it can't do you any harm to be in bed with Google. For a detailed approach to maximising your effectiveness using Google Adwords check out *Google Adwords That Work: 7 secrets for cashing in with the world's no. 1 search engine*, also by Jon Smith.

50

I'll make you number 1!

The dangers of SEO/AdWords 'specialists'

Where there's an opportunity, there's an opportunist... The tools and techniques being offered by SEO 'specialists' are those contained here, and are probably not even this exhaustive...

An expensive business

Web developers, designers and engineers have enjoyed a hallowed ground immunity for many years. The impenetrable black art of website creation has proven to be a fortress to which most of us mere mortals simply do not hold a key. We've been reliant upon their views in terms of the look, feel and design of our websites for so long that we've got used to it – and they've got used to it too.

I'm not for a moment suggesting that web developers are without value. Far from it; they offer a service for which you pay and, more often than not, you'll receive a decent product in return. But they are looking to expand their portfolio of incomes, and what better way than to hit existing customers with extra products and services – namely SEO: 'We've built your site, now let us take it to the next level...'

Outsourced SEO can cost anywhere between £100 and £1000 a month – the question is, do your returns justify this expenditure? How much of it can you now do in-house and, more importantly, how much do you want to do in-house?

Taking the hit

Conversely, now you're armed with the knowledge, the techniques and the lingo, it might actually prove cost-effective to employ a third party on a monthly basis to look after your SEO while you get on with whatever it is that you do best, depending on your turnover and staffing levels. Only you will truly know the answer to this. For some businesses it does make financial sense to employ a third party. Now you know the questions to ask, the language to use and you have a mental checklist of all the things you should, quite rightly, expect to be delivered. The balance has altered. Whilst you may opt to remain a customer, you are now a very informed customer.

Here's an idea for you

Possibly morally wrong, but this is business, not charity. Take a look on the web or get recommendations through contacts at the firms offering SEO improvements. What are they offering? What assurances are you receiving? What will they do, as a sweetener, to get you involved? Without fail insist on at least a month of demonstrable improvement to your listings before parting with cash, and sit on them to make sure they are still looking after your site once that money has changed hands.

51

Is this working?

User testing to monitor your search results

Testing and re-testing is fundamentally important to the success of your search engine marketing. Companies that choose not to test may as well sit there and smoke £20 notes...

The truth hurts

User testing does take up time. It can cost (but nowhere near as much as the cost of failure). Your testers' comments, at best, will make you disappointed and at worst will mean rethinking your entire search-engine marketing strategy, but done professionally and continually you will reap many rewards. User testing must go outside the walls of those with a vested interest in the success of the site. If you all share the same paymaster there is bound to be some bias and that is not going to give you the honest and reliable feedback you need from Joe Public, from the girl on the street with nothing better to do on a Tuesday afternoon...

What is to be done?

Testing can be done on a shoestring and anyone who knows what the Internet is will do as a tester. Prepare a brief for your testers; introduce them to the company and the website and explain what you want from them. Set specific search tasks – for example, if you run a website specialising in villa holidays, you'll want one tester to be searching for destinations ('villa Cyprus', 'villa Spain', etc.) and another tester to be searching for industry ('villa', 'holiday', 'self-catering', etc.). Compile the results – your position on the page, the position of competitors, your AdWords campaign listing position if applicable, etc.

By all means have a number of testers working on the same search terms, but treat them like defendants in a police interview – don't let them meet and don't let them compare notes. Only when the testing is completed should you then see what, if any, correlation can be drawn.

If possible have testers around the world, or at least in the UK and US, as the results returned can vary drastically depending on the IP address of the web browser making the search. If you do trade (or wish to trade) with US customers, this is essential.

Here's an idea for you

If you have a set of testers available when you're developing a new keyword-specific destination page, get them to give you their comments about whether the page 'answers the question'. If, for example, you are selling a new skin cream high in aloe vera ask your testers if the page does what it should – explaining the importance of aloe vera, why your cream is better than the others on the market and where/how users can order. This third-party viewpoint can be invaluable. Pay attention to any other comments testers might have about colour, layout, ease of use, etc. They might all focus on what may seem like a banal point – 'I don't really like that shade of green', 'Looks a bit like suchandsuch.com', etc. – but this is what user testing is all about. By fixing the little problems you will make your site great. Ultimately this is what will convert users, who find you via Google, into consumers.

52

I am/am not king of the hill

A word of warning

Take a look at me now! King of the hill, number 1 on a global search for any keyword you care to think of – an unstoppable sex machine. I own the web...

Who's your daddy?

So, with your new-found SEO obsession it's all come together and you're sitting pretty on the number 1 spot. Well, you can be assured that someone else covets your space and they're going to be looking for ways to beat you down. Do not lose sight of your goals, ever. The web is constantly changing. New sites pop up every day and old sites drop off, without so much as a by your leave, but the number 1 spot is the most coveted. Your competitors covet it with as much, if not more, venom than you once did – all those weeks or months ago.

Equally, search engine optimisation takes time. This is not a quick fix overnight tweak that means, come tomorrow morning, your website is more popular than ebay, or Amazon or YouTube. For a start it's going to take a few weeks for Google to send the Googlebot to your site (whether you request it or not) – there are millions of sites out there craving the attention of Google et al., and the process takes time. Don't lose heart. If you play by the rules, increase the number of in-bound links from relevant sites, keep your site updated and relevant and constantly monitor, measure and react then your site will rank highly. Patience, in business, is something we all lack.

Hang on! Yesterday I was on page 1, today I'm on page 13!

Google, and to a lesser extent all of the other search engines, are also tweaking their service, constantly. It is very clear that Google alters the algorithm once too many people cotton on to what makes certain sites rank highly (which has led inevitably to abuse). Five years ago it was all the rage to have as many reciprocal links as you could; now Google is only interested in in-bound or backwards links. In six months the algorithm will alter again, and all we can do is adapt and try to keep up. The important thing is that all of the ideas here will help you rank highly on Google and all of the other search engines and continue to do so in the years to come. It is your responsibility as a website owner to keep up to date with what's hot and what's not.

Here's an idea for you

When you've been improving how you rank with Google for about a year, it's time
to take stock and more importantly look towards the new year and the business
challenges it will bring. However your performance has been, type in your most
treasured keyword, find the first reference to your site and print off the page – this
is your baseline. For the next twelve months you either need to maintain that
position or improve on it. Print out the page, stick it up on the wall and spend each
and every day employing these techniques and rising up the rankings.

Index